19.99
YP
By t
Deb. 2000

What I Wish I'd
Known in
HIGH
SCHOOL

What I Wish I'd Known in HIGH SCHOOL

REVISED EDITION

JOHN BYTHEWAY

SHADOW MOUNTAIN
SALT LAKE CITY, UTAH

To the family members,
faculty, and students of
Columbine High School

Library of Congress Cataloging-in-Publication Number: 99-26399

Printed in the United States of America

10   9   8   7   6   5   4   3   2   1   6402

CLASS SCHEDULE

ORIENTATION   1
Welcome to school!

SOCIAL SCENE 101   7
Popular. Yes, popular. This chapter is like, so totally popular, okay?

SELF-ESTEEM 101   19
I just wanna be happy. Is that so wrong?

PERSISTENCE 101   39
Finding the prize inside

DISCIPLINE 101   59
What my braces taught me about life

PERSONAL FINANCE 101   75
Get a job!

ROMANCE 101   93
What love's got to do with it

PREPARATION 101   111
How to get opportunity to knock you over

INDEX   131

ORIENTATION

Welcome to school!

Properly, we should read for power. Man reading should be man intensely alive. The book should be a ball of light in one's hand.

—*Ezra Pound*

Hey, who are you? What are you doing? Put me down. You're a teenager! Teenagers don't read books! Shouldn't you be hanging out at the mall, or watching TV? Shouldn't you be out in the parking lot kicking a little spherical bag into the air with your foot? Haven't you heard that reading is boring? Go play some video games, okay? Put me down, kid, you're wrinkling my pages.

Ctrl-Alt-Del. Bzzzt. Bzzzt, static. Beep. Static. Click.

Hello? Are you still there? Sorry about that first paragraph; I'm not sure where that came from. Hi. My name is John, and I'm the author of this book, and you must be the reader! Hey, this is great! I'm glad you're here. I've never met you, but I'm impressed already. You see, whoever said that up there was right: Teenagers don't read books. At least, that's what a publisher once told me. Obviously, that publisher has never met you. So far you've read only two paragraphs, but you've already distinguished yourself as a very unusual person. You're

3

different! You're doing something that most people your age aren't doing.

I'm really not quite sure why you're still reading, but I'm glad you are. Perhaps you've already learned that the key to having a great life and living your dreams isn't found in guzzling pop, snarfing Doritos, and vegging in front of the television. Perhaps you know that the key to a great life is found in learning and growing and discovering. And perhaps you've already learned that all the wisdom, the wonder, and the adventures of the world are magically preserved in the pages of books. Someone once explained the power of reading like this:

The more you read, the more you know.
The more you know, the smarter you grow.
The smarter you grow, the stronger your voice
In expressing your view, or making your
       choice. . .

Knowledge is power! and that's what reading is all about. There is an unbelievably large universe of information out there, and you can explore it because *you can read.* Books are like time machines that can take you to another time and place in an instant. (I hope you will read many books after this one—I'll even recommend a few.) It's like Walt Disney once said, "There is more treasure in books than in all the pirates' loot on Treasure Island . . . and best of all, you can enjoy these riches every day of your life."

With so many millions of books to choose from, you may be wondering why I wrote this book. Good question. To be honest, I've been writing this book ever since I was sixteen. I didn't actually sit down and pound it out on the word processor until recently, but I've been trying to find the right words to explain certain things for a long time. I remember one high school day when I felt a little frustrated. (I'm sure that's never happened to you, right?) I ended up at the school library looking for a book that hadn't been written. The book I wanted wasn't about math or history or social studies or any academic subject. I wanted answers about subjects teachers don't normally talk about. For example: Why the obsession with being popular? What's up with that? Why do some people treat you differently when they're alone than when they're with their friends? Why do I feel good some days and bad other days? Am I moody? Is there life after high school? How can I be happy? And on and on and on.

What I've tried to do is write the book I was looking for all those years ago, with all the things I wish I'd known when I was in high school. I wanted a book that would help me understand what was going on and make me feel like I was going to make it.

I want *this* book to be that kind of book for you. I want it to make you feel good and to help you realize that you can do and be anything you set your heart on. Can I say that again? *You can do and be anything you set your heart on!* And I want to help you do it. Of course, you'll need to read all the way to the end. I mean, don't just read the first chapter and quit. I'll try to leave out the parts that people skip.

Specifically, I have three goals for you as you read. It is my hope that you will have fun, learn things, and make changes. Everybody likes to have fun, and so do I.

So I want to make this book fun to read. I also want you to learn things, the kind of things that will make you a better person. And finally, I want you to make changes. In reality, by itself this book can't help you at all. It can help you only if you put it down and go out and do what you've learned. So the second goal (after having fun) is to know what to do, and the third is to *do* what you *know!* In the end, if this book does any good, it will be because of you.

My name is John, and I wrote this little book. But from now on, I don't want you to think of this as a book. I want you to think of it as a letter—a letter from a friend who has great respect for you and what you can become. Is that okay with you? I hope so. I'm still young. I mean, I was a teenager not too long ago. In fact, if we met, I'll bet you'd look at me and say, "Man, I thought you were old." (I hear that from teenagers all the time.) I remember my teenage years very well. And I wish I'd had a book like this back when I was in high school.

One more thing. Unless you just picked this up from the library, *this is your book,* so treat it that way. I hope you'll use a highlighter when you read. Highlight what you like or what you have questions about. Underline, write notes in the margin, or whatever. That way, when you thumb through it at another time, you'll see what stood out to you before. If you'll do that much, I'll try to make it as interesting, informative, and useful as possible. Deal? Deal.

I know you could be doing a lot of other things right now. Thanks for choosing to read. Dive in and have fun. And hey—don't worry if you wrinkle the pages.

First Period
SOCIAL SCENE 101

Popular. Yes, popular. This chapter is like, so totally popular, okay?

*Popularity ends on yearbook day,
but respect lasts forever.*

W hat does it mean to be popular? I'll tell you. I don't know. Fact is, it's different wherever you go. Some people who are popular in one school might not be in another. Some extracurricular activities are popular in some schools and not in others. No doubt you know exactly what the cool things are in *your* school: the right things to wear, the right things to say, the right music groups to listen to, the right activities to try out for, and on and on and on.

Who figures all this out? Is there some "Committee of Coolness" that meets after school and decides what is acceptable and what isn't? Does anyone write down what they decide, or does everyone just know? Do television and movie producers decide for us? Do those most admired or most visible in our school have an influence?

Are you getting the feeling that we're all just following someone and we don't know who? Scary.

Well, what does "being popular" mean, then? I think

you already know. Simply put, being popular means that a lot of people know who you are, and maybe that they admire you for your self-assurance.

But there's another trait that is much better than popularity. It's more valuable and long lasting, but many high school students aren't smart or alert enough to recognize it. I'll show you. Think really hard for a minute: Who are the people you most respect in your school? (Not the most *popular*, but the most *respected*.) Chances are, they're the ones who are friendly to everyone. They're nice to those who are in "their group," but also to those who are not. They're not "two-faced."

Perhaps you've watched one of these people and noticed how he or she seems to be everyone's friend. And maybe something inside you said, "That's the right way to be; it's the way people *should* be, and I would like to be that way too." When you look up to someone like that, it's called respect. That's what we really ought to be looking for here, isn't it? Respect. Stay with me, and I'll tell you how to earn it.

Have you ever had a TV dinner? I'm not asking if you ate the Magnavox, I'm asking if you've ever had the kind of TV dinner you cook in the microwave. Have you noticed how the tray is shaped into little compartments? There's a place for the turkey and stuffing, a place for the peas, a place for the mashed potatoes (no matter how long you nuke the dinner in the microwave, the potatoes never seem to get hot in the center), and a place for the cranberry sauce (this stuff gets so hot it melts your fork and burns your tongue, and then you can't taste anything for the rest of the meal . . . which is probably a good thing).

Sometimes we treat people like the food in a TV dinner. We don't cram them in the microwave, but we do put them into compartments. I don't know the names for the "compartments" in your school, but here are some that I've heard:

"These are the jocks, these are the loners, these are the rockers, these are the cowboys, these are the skaters, these are the grunges, these are the popular people, like, okay?" And it's as if someone is standing over the tray saying, "All right, nobody move! Hey—you can't talk to him, you're not popular (whack, whack). Get back in your place!" Sound familiar? Putting people into compartments is mean, and it can hurt. People who know who they are and are comfortable with being themselves don't do that. Being popular may be nice, but being respected means you're mature enough to see over the walls that divide people into compartments.

Anybody can put up walls. That's easy. I mean, if you're only nice to the people who are nice to you, you are pretty ordinary, because everybody does that. And if you only say "hi" in the hall to the people who say "hi" to you, what are you doing more than anyone else? No doubt you know people who are different when they're alone than when they're with their friends, right? Maybe they'll speak to you if they're alone, but with their group they act like they've never seen you before. And you walk away saying, "what-EVER!"

Do you want to be popular? Or better yet, do you want to be respected? Then no matter how others treat you, be the same toward them at all times, not "double minded" or "two-faced." This makes life a whole lot easier because you don't have to put on a new personality depending on which group you're with. That's too much work! When you're always the same, you're always yourself, no matter who you're talking to—it's much better! (Besides, being two-faced gets expensive. You have to buy two hair dryers, two curling irons, two toothbrushes, and fit two mirrors in your locker.)

You know there are people in your school who don't have many friends. Some of them are the brunt of every joke and get teased a lot. What can you do about it? Well, when you see someone walking down the hall, eyes on the ground, no friends in sight, you be the one to say "hi." Even if all you say is "hi," it can make a difference, because actions speak louder than words. Saying "hi" also says, "You're an important person, whether you're in my 'compartment' or not. I'm not ashamed to recognize you, in front of all these people, as a worthwhile human being."

Does that scare you? Did I just hear you say, "No way"? Are you afraid you'll lose friends? Well, just try it and see. I'm not saying you should invite this person over to your house or buy a "best friend" necklace. But Ann Landers once said, "Keep in mind that the true measure of an individual is how he treats a person who can do him absolutely no good." Try being respectful to those who can't do anything for you, and watch how your self-respect and respect from others will grow.

I've heard stories of young people who were about to go home and take their own lives, but changed their mind when someone said "hi." Sometimes a simple "hi" from you—yes, you—can really make a person's day. And if *that's* true, just imagine what a difference you could make if you were to call the person by name. Try it sometime. Find out the name of someone who could use a friendly comment. (I'll bet you can think of someone right now.) Next time you see that person in the hall, say, "Hi, _____ (insert name here)."

Let's imagine it happening. One day, you're walking down the hall, and you see someone who doesn't quite belong. Maybe she has been labeled as a "loner." So you say, "Hi, Chris," and you keep walking as if it were no big deal. Just a casual "Hi, Chris," and you keep right on going. Now, what is Chris doing? Imagine Chris's thoughts echoing like in the movies: "How did she know my name?" And you, my friend, have just made a miracle. Someone was just made to feel important . . . by you. You're still walking down the hall, and Chris is watching you walk away, with a confused look on her face. You never know what burdens your classmates might be carrying, and a simple, friendly "hi" can make a lonely person's world turn from darkness to day.

I watched a young man in my school do something one day that broke all the rules of how popular people are supposed to act. We were all socializing in a part of the building we called "jock hall." This was where all the "upper-crust" people hung out. Rodney, a tough kid and an all-star hockey player, walked down the stairs on the left. Instead of joining the social people in the hall, Rodney walked by the doorway of the Special Education room. A teacher was wheeling a severely mentally and physically handicapped boy into the hall. I watched out of the corner of my eye as Rodney, who later went on to play hockey at Cornell University, knelt on the hard floor and said to this student, "Hi, how are you doing today?" The boy couldn't even respond—but you could see a brightness in his eyes because he knew someone was being nice to him. Rodney smiled, patted him on the arm, and continued down the hall. I was amazed. I had just seen something I never would have expected. But inside I knew, like you know, that there was something really right about what I had just seen.

Of course, you need to be careful about this. It has to be real, or, better said, *you* have to be real. This isn't something to *do,* this is something to *be.* If you walk up to someone and say, "Hi, I'd like to make you my personal charity project for the month," it will probably backfire. It has to come from inside.

If we change only how we act on the outside, our *behavior,* we might seem condescending and rude. If we really desire from the inside out to help people, we have to change our *nature.* Then our actions will naturally follow—we won't have to fake it.

Now, perhaps you're a student leader in your school: a student-body officer, a cheerleader, a class officer, or something else. Good for you! That's great. No doubt that takes a lot of work and a lot of energy, and hopefully, it's a lot of fun, too. You are in a great position to make miracles happen in your school. Make that monogrammed sweater or letterman's jacket mean something! Don't let it be a sign that says, "Go away!" Let it be an invitation that says, "Come and talk to me! How's

school? What's up in your life? You goin' to the game?"
As a student leader, you're looked up to. People will follow you, so lead! Make it the cool thing to do to be kind
and accepting to everyone. As the saying goes, "It's nice
to be important, but it's more important to be nice."

Now, there's one more thing that makes this whole
idea a little complicated. It's called boys and girls
together in the same place and everyone trying to figure
out who likes whom. Sometimes, if we're not careful,
we can "train" others *not* to be nice. Let me give you an
example: Let's say a girl tries to be nice to a boy and he
assumes, "Oh . . . she must like me," when the girl was
only trying to be friendly. This can cause so many problems for the girl that she may decide, "Forget this! Every
time I try to be nice to a guy, he misunderstands, and
then I have to tell him I just want to be friends, and then
he might say I'm stuck up, and YUCK . . . this just isn't
worth it, so I just won't talk to guys." Can you see how
that can happen? We train people not to be nice.

So what's the point? The point is, chill! Let people
be nice just to be nice. If a guy or girl likes you in an
"I'd-like-to-go-out-with-you" way, you'll know. People
know how to send that message, too. Why don't we all
just calm down, chill out, or whatever the latest phrase
is, and be kind.

If, after all this, you still want to be popular, I'll tell
you how. Forget it. Stop trying. Be you. Focus on being
the best you can be, and the rest will happen. You will
be respected. It is much better to be respected than to be
popular. Oooh, that sounded profound, can I say that
again? I might even put it in italics for emphasis. *It is*

better to be respected than to be popular. Who knows, maybe you'll be both. You'll be popular because you're respected. You won't have to go off to college remembering regrets from high school.

Besides, popularity can be a fleeting thing. I remember in junior high school observing some of my classmates who were so confident, so popular. They wore all the right clothes and said all the right things. I watched them a lot, I guess because I kind of admired their confidence. I wanted to be like that.

Years passed. I remember another day as a senior in high school when I thought about some of those people I had looked up to in junior high. Where had they gone? They weren't in the limelight anymore. Something had happened. They were the ones who started dating before everyone else, who started partying before everyone else. They got ahead of themselves, and many of them blew it. They made mistakes and damaged their reputations and got involved in things that took them down. And it seemed like another group of students— the ones who were a little quieter in junior high—kind of stepped up into their spots and took over. Interesting.

Anyway, if you're not "popular," please, don't spend one calorie of energy worrying about it. It's not worth it, and it's not that big a deal. There is life after high school. Think about it! Most of your life is *after* high school! And your high school experience is not a forecast for your life. Spend your energy on more important things.

In the meantime, do the best you can at being you. That shouldn't be too hard—you've been doing it since you were born. People don't gain respect by imitating others; they're popular because they're comfortable being themselves. Make sense? I hope so. As one of my favorite authors, Og Mandino, has written:

"Be yourself. Try to be anything else but your genuine self, even if you deceive the entire world, and you will be ten thousand times worse than nothing. . . . You have been blessed with special skills that are yours alone. Use them, whatever they may be, and forget about wearing another's hat. A talented chariot driver can win gold and renown with his skills. Let him pick figs and he would starve. No one can take your place! Realize this and be yourself. You have no obligation to succeed. You have only the obligation to be true to yourself. Do the very best that you can, in the things you do best, and you will know, in thy soul, that you are the greatest success in the world" (*The Greatest Success in the World,* Bantam Books, 1981, p. 94).

I love that! I want to change one word, though. "You have no obligation to be *popular!* You have only the obligation to be true to yourself." Live your life according to the things you most value, and you'll earn respect. I'll say it one more time: It is better to be respected than to be popular. Popularity ends on yearbook day, but respect can last forever.

As for high school, you have three or four years to do it and the rest of your life to think about it. When you graduate, many will grab your yearbook and try to summarize your high school experience in a sentence or two. Which tribute would you rather see? One like this:

"I didn't know you very well, but I always respected

you for the way you lived your life and the way you treated others. Some people are only nice to those who will help them climb the social ladder, but you were different. You were nice to people who couldn't improve your social standing at all. You were nice because it was right, even to the loners. One of those was me. Thank you for being a friend when I felt like I didn't have one."

Or, you could get one that said this:

"No way! You were like, so totally popular, okay? It was so funny when you totally dogged that loner guy! Stay rad! Like, call me!"

Think about it. Thanks for listening, and I'll see you in Second Period. Don't be late!

Second Period

SELF-ESTEEM 101

I just wanna be happy.
Is that so wrong?

The time to be happy is now. The place to be happy is here. The way to be happy is to make others so.

—*Robert G. Ingersoll*

Are you happy?

Please answer that question before you go on. In fact, I'd like you to write your answer in the blank below. Think deep down, imagine the "Final Jeopardy" music playing, and read the question again slowly.

Are you happy? _____

Well, obviously I can't see it from here; what did you put? Most teenagers won't write anything down, probably because they're not excited about their answer. When I meet people, especially teens, I love to ask them that question. *Are you happy?* Sadly, most of the time their eyes drop to the floor, their face contorts, and the response is either "sort of" or "yeah, I guess" or simply "no."

We have more time, more money, more information, more entertainment, more music, more computers, more books, more gadgets, more electronics, more cable channels, better nutrition, better stereos, better science, better hospitals, nicer cars, faster roller blades than ever before—we ought to be the happiest people in the world! But the fact is, many teenagers, and adults as well, are simply not happy. What's the problem?

Maybe we think we're *supposed* to be happy, *all the time.* If we were *always* happy, perhaps we'd get used to it and take it for granted. Maybe we need to be sad once in a while to appreciate the happy times.

Now, at this point you may be saying, "Hey, give me a break! I don't know why I'm not happy; that's why I picked up this book!" Well, it's time for your author to make a confession. As a fifteen-year-old, I was sitting in an assembly at school, and the speaker said, "Raise your hand if you're happy." You know what? I didn't. I just stared at the floor and thought about my pimples and my social status. Our happiness is often closely related to how we feel about ourselves.

If you're like me, you may be asking the same teenage question I did: "Why do I feel like I'm riding an emotional roller coaster? Why do I have so many ups and downs?" Well, some of those things are just a part of growing up. And growing up takes time. However, it may also be that you're building your foundation for happiness in the wrong place. Young or old, we *must* build on solid ground or we'll never feel stable.

REAL ESTATE AND REAL ESTEEM

Let's say you're going to build a house, and you're looking for a nice piece of land. Your real-estate agent fumbles through his listings and says, "Say, I know a great area, and it's really cheap!"

"What's it called?" you ask.

"Landslide Hills."

"Why is it called that!?"

"Well, because, uh, one day you'll be living on the north side of the street, and you'll hear a  loud rumbling noise, a few pictures will fall off the walls, and then you'll be on the south side of the street."

"Uh, no, I don't think so."

"Well, let's see, I have some property next to a big river. The Petersons used to live there . . . yup, 1016 Backstroke Drive."

"Are they still there?"

"No, they floated downstream last spring. Now they're at 1216 Backstroke Drive."

"Wow. What else have you got?"

"I believe two homes are up for sale on the fault line, let's see, yes! One home at 907 Achy Quaky Heart Circle, and one at 486 D. Fault Drive."

"Hmmm. Do you have anything with a better foundation?"

"How firm a foundation?"

"I want something that will remain standing through rainstorms and floods and winds . . . you know, something rock solid."

"Oh—you want to build on a rock."

"Yes, of course; I thought you would take that for granite."

(We're gonna break the fun meter today, folks.)

When you're looking to build something important, something that you want to remain standing, you want to build on solid ground. But it's especially tempting to build our feelings about ourselves on not-so-solid ground. Our world tells us that happiness comes from fame, wealth, awards, trophies, appearance, status, and so on. All that stuff looks really nice, but it's actually risky real estate! If you build there, you're taking your chances. Hop in the truck, buckle up, and let's check out a few of these spots. You'll see what I mean.

LANDSLIDE HILLS—THE WAY OTHERS TREAT US

Hmmm, this looks nice. We could build our happiness on our friends, our fame, or on the way others treat us. Aren't friends great? Choose your friends wisely, they say, because friends can make such a difference in your life. It's the best feeling in the world to have good friends who make you feel like you belong.

Some of my favorite high school memories didn't happen at school, but just driving around with my friends. I can't even remember what we did half the time. We would laugh, go places, eat, visit girls; it was so much fun—good, clean fun. So maybe that's it: Happiness and self-esteem come from friends. That's where we'll build. Can we stop reading the book now because we've figured it out?

Well, no. Friendships are great, but friendships can slip and slide and avalanche away, too. A foundation built on friendships is a good temporary foundation, but it's not the best. Some friendships can be more like rivalries. One friend of mine had a landslide in her friendship neighborhood. She expressed it like this:

"One day they're your friend, and the next day they're your enemy. It's like they're saying, 'Okay, today

I'll be your friend, but tomorrow, I'm going to tell everyone what you told me about so and so, and you'll wonder why I'm trying to ruin your life. Then on another day, I'll be your friend again and act like nothing happened. Your job, of course, is to forgive me every time, because no matter what, it's your fault.'"

Yuck. Thus the familiar saying, "With friends like that, who needs enemies?" I suppose these things are ordinary in young friendships, but you, my friend, are not ordinary. And someone as extraordinary as you must be an extraordinary friend. We'll keep our good friendships, but we'd better not build on Landslide Hills, or we'll be comin' down the mountain. Let's pack up and move out—fasten your seat belt and pass the Twinkies. Okay, where else should we look? Let's check out the river!

BACKSTROKE DRIVE—OUR APPEARANCE

Hey, this is nice! Backstroke Drive looks really attractive. Why don't we try building our happiness on our appearance? You know, our clothes, our looks, our "image." Kind of tempting, huh?

Personal appearance becomes very important in the teenage years. If mirrors could talk, I'll bet they'd say they see teenagers the most. Teenagers want answers to questions like, How do I look to others? Do people think I'm good looking? Do *I* think I'm good looking? Does that special someone in Biology

good looking? Am I too skinny, chubby, tall,
de, narrow, etc, etc., etc.?

rtunately, the media has trained us to appreci-
few body types. I think Leo Tolstoy said it well:
"It is amazing how complete is the delusion that beauty
is goodness."

Sometimes what the world portrays as beautiful isn't
even real. A few years ago, actress Michelle Pfeiffer was
featured on the front cover of *Esquire* magazine. The
caption under her photo read, "What Michelle Pfeiffer
Needs . . . Is Absolutely Nothing." The truth is, she
needed a little help to look that good. Allen Litchfield
reveals the rest of the story:

"But another magazine, *Harper's*, offered proof in
their edition the following month that even the
Beautiful People need a little help. *Harper's* had
obtained the photo retoucher's bill for Pfeiffer's picture
on the *Esquire* cover. The retouchers charged $1,525 to
render the following services: 'Clean up complexion,
soften smile line, trim chin, soften line under earlobe,
add hair, add forehead to create better line, and soften
neck muscles.' The editor of *Harper's* printed the story
because we are, he said, 'constantly faced with perfec-
tion in magazines; this is to remind the reader . . .
there's a difference between real life and art'" (*Sharing
the Light,* Deseret Book, 1993, p. 107).

This is why you shouldn't be comparing your yearbook or driver's license photographs with the magazine
cover faces. The photographer who is shooting your picture is getting paid minimum wage, is bored, in a hurry,

and may even hate you. Little wonder your picture comes out looking awful.

Some famous people have so much retouching done, if you saw them in person you wouldn't even recognize them. In fact, supermodel Cindy Crawford is actually a 5' 2" dockworker from Cleveland (just kidding). When I was an acne-faced teenager, I wish I'd had an artist to "clean up my complexion" each morning, but I didn't.

We all know that people should be valued for what's inside, not for the package they came in. Besides, with time the package will change. We don't love our grandmas because they are supermodels; we love them because of the quality of their hearts.

Yup, better not build on Backstroke Drive. If we do, our self-esteem will float away like the other homes built on the riverbank. Back in the truck, Chuck. Now, what was the other place the agent mentioned?

ACHY QUAKY HEART CIRCLE OR D. FAULT DRIVE— OUR ACCOMPLISHMENTS

Why don't we base our self-esteem on our accomplishments? Yeah, that's it. If I can just get lots of trophies and lots of awards and lots of recognition, then I'll feel great, right? Why don't we build our happiness here? Because it's earthquake city, that's why. We believe in setting and achieving goals and everything else, and we know these things can help us feel happy. But we're looking for the *best* place to build, not just a good place.

You see, if you judge yourself solely by your accomplishments, you may never be happy. You will always be able to find someone who can do more or better, and you may be tempted to compare yourself with them.

A few years ago, I was invited to speak to a group of sixty-six contestants in a beauty pageant. The winner would be crowned and go on to the Miss America pageant in Atlantic City. Being young and single, I thought about it for, oh, about 1.5 nanoseconds, and then said, "Okay! Um, what should I talk about?"

The woman in charge responded: "Give 'em a motivational talk, make them laugh a little, and help them not to feel so much pressure. They get a lot of pressure from boyfriends and parents. I just want them to relax."

I was supposed to give my talk the day before the pageant began. What do you say to a group like this at a time like this? I mean, I was glad I was giving the talk—as a single guy, I wouldn't miss the chance—but what should I say?

I prepared a lot of ideas, you know, like, "It's not whether you win or lose" and "If at first you don't succeed . . ." Finally, I remembered a conversation between a coach and a member of the Jamaican bobsled team in the movie *Cool Runnings*. I loved the whole movie, but I especially loved this brief dialogue. I think it was my favorite part.

Here's the scene: It was the night before the team's third and final run. The gold medal was on the line, and the pressure was on. Coach Irving Blitzer (played by John Candy) was on the way out of the team's hotel room when Derice Bannock (played by Leon) stopped him:

Derice: Hey, Coach!

Coach Blitzer: Yeah?

Derice: I have to ask you a question.

Coach Blitzer: Sure.

Derice: But, you don't have to answer if you don't want. I mean, I want you to, but if you can't, I understand.

Coach Blitzer: You want to know why I cheated, right?

Derice: Yes, I do.

Coach Blitzer: That's a fair question. It's quite simple, really. I had to win. You see, Derice, I'd made winning my whole life. And when you make winning your whole life, you have to keep on winning, no matter what. D'you understand that?

Derice: No, I don't understand, Coach. You had two gold medals! You had it all!

Coach Blitzer: Derice, a *gold medal is a wonderful thing. But if you're not enough without it, you'll never be enough with it.*

After sharing this dialogue with the sixty-six contestants, I repeated the last line again, but this time I changed a few words. (I thought this was a pretty gutsy move, if I do say so myself.) "Tonight, one of you will walk out of here with a crown on your head. The audience will stand and applaud, and we'll all be very happy for you. Just remember, the title you'll get is a wonderful thing. But if you're not enough without it, you'll never be enough with it."

So there you have it. Accomplishments are great. They

bring a temporary high, but time passes! Trophies get dusty, people forget that last shot at the buzzer, and all your glory days fade away. Yeah, accomplishments are nice, but Coach Blitzer was right: If you're not enough without them, you'll never be enough with them. Besides, if you spend your whole life in a quest for self-aggrandizement, running around shouting, "Look at me, look at me," you will annoy more people than you impress. You want to be valued for *you,* not for your looks or your accomplishments!

Many things make us feel happy for a while, but only a few things can help us be happy for a long time. I'm not talking about the perma-grin-on-your-face happiness that makes you want to hug the bus driver and the grocery clerk, but a quieter kind of happiness, a content feeling. Maybe the best way to describe that feeling is "inner peace." Where can we turn for peace? Well, not to D. Fault Drive or Achy Quaky Heart Circle. In fact, if you build on Achy Quaky, all you'll get is shake and bakey. (Ah, there's nothing like fine poetry.)

So far we've checked out three places, and none of them checked out. There are hundreds of other places where we could look for a foundation for our happiness, but we're about to run out of gas! Where is the best place? We want a strong, durable foundation that will last for a lifetime.

GET A PLACE ON THE ROCK

When Coach Blitzer said, "If you're not enough without it, you'll never be enough with it," Derice responded, "How will I know if I'm enough?" Folks, there's the big question.

All of the foundations we've talked about so far—how others treat us, our appearance, and our accomplishments—have a common flaw. They all use the outside-in approach. If others treat me nice, then I'll be happy. If people say I look great, then I'll be happy. If I can win lots of trophies and awards, then I'll know I'm worth something, because somebody out there said so.

When we depend on things outside of ourselves to tell us what we're worth, we're in trouble. There are all kinds of voices in the world, but the problem is, those voices can be very fickle. One day they'll be giving you praise, and another day they'll be saying, "You'll never make it" and "You're not good enough." Turn the negative voices off and listen to the voice on the inside. That still, small voice will confirm that happiness is an inside-out job.

The gift I wish I could give to you and every young reader of this book is the realization of how much you have to offer on the inside. You may not see it yet, and that's okay, but believe me, it's in there. If I were a better writer, perhaps I could find a way to help you see what you are capable of becoming. I guess you'll just have to trust me. You need to see yourself as a worthwhile person before other people's saying you are worthwhile will do any good.

"Inside" things are often called spiritual things. Many people find their rock in their religious beliefs. Perhaps you do too. Abraham Lincoln once said, "It is hard to make a man miserable when he feels he is worthy of himself and claims kindred to that Great God who made him." When we sense our relationship to God, it

31

gives us a sense of increased worth. You've probably seen this message on a child's T-shirt: "I know I'm somebody 'cause God don't make no junk." Bad grammar, but a nice idea.

Marianne Williamson wrote:

"We ask ourselves, who am I to be brilliant, gorgeous, talented, fabulous? Actually, who are you not to be?

"You are a child of God. . . . We were all meant to shine as children do. We were born to make manifest the glory of God that is within us. It is not just in some of us; it's in everyone! And as we let our own light shine, we unconsciously give other people permission to do the same. As we're liberated from our own fear, our presence automatically liberates others" (*A Return to Love,* Harper Collins, 1993, pp. 183–189).

The Academy-Award-winning musical *Fiddler on the Roof* tells the story of Jewish Russian peasants struggling to survive amidst persecution and other hardships. What was their rock? The main character, Tevye, explains, "Because of our traditions [Jewish belief and culture], every man knows who he is, and what God expects him to become." Knowing who you are is the key.

Someone who can lose the pageant five times in a row and still hold her head high knows that although she lost on the outside, she's "enough" on the inside. A guy who's been cut from the basketball team every year he's tried out may on the outside look like a loser, and he may even feel like a loser for a while, but he knows on the inside that the world hasn't seen anything yet. He still has more to offer.

Bouncing back like that is not an easy thing to do when you're a teenager. And this is one of the main reasons being a teenager can be hard, because you're still searching for a solid foundation. Some people say, "He's having an identity crisis," or, "She hasn't found herself." I believe you will find yourself, if you keep trying, and the day will come that you will know that you're "enough." And that realization won't come from the outside, it will come from the inside.

WHAT IS SELF-ESTEEM, ANYWAY?

Self-esteem is when you go jogging in the winter and steam rises from your sweats. Oh, wait. That's self-steam—never mind.

You've probably heard someone give a speech in which the first thing he or she did was read from the dictionary. I'm afraid we're going to have to do that too, because thousands of writers have used the same words to mean different things. Before we go on, we'd better decide what we mean by "self-esteem."

Should we say that having good self-esteem means that we'll always feel good about ourselves? Yes. I mean, no. Well, maybe. Wait a sec . . . I mean, we'd better not. Because, if you *always* feel good about yourself, there's probably something wrong. Sometimes you might feel bad for a good reason.

Throughout your life, you will have moments when you want to be a better person. You may feel like you're not living up to your potential, or you may feel like you're not living up to the high standards you've set for yourself. You might see someone you admire or want to be like. You might notice things in your behavior that you want to change, and that might even make you feel a little down. Those moments aren't necessarily bad. There's something deep inside all of us that pushes us to be better. We should all be careful not to become too satisfied or complacent with where we are now. You can be a better person. And you *will* be better!

So, let's go back to the definition thing. I think that self-worth and self-esteem are two different things. Look at the graph below, and I'll tell you what I mean.

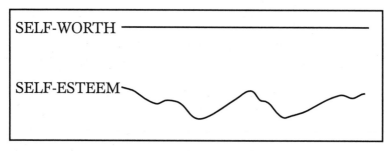

Self-Worth = What you are worth

Self-Esteem = How you feel about what you are worth

For this book, we're going to say that your self-worth is what you are worth. It never changes. It remains constant. (It doesn't matter whether you *think* you're worth something or not. You are. So cork it and keep reading.) Your self-worth is constant, like a rock.

Your self-*esteem,* on the other hand, is how you *feel* about what you're worth. It's how you "esteem" or estimate your self-worth. It can go up and down, especially if you attach it to flimsy-foundation, outside things like appearance, accomplishments, and how others treat you. See the difference?

Well, what are you worth, then? No one knows. It's impossible to calculate. No one can tell just by looking at you how you will make the world a better place. So let's just say that your self-worth is your *unlimited potential*—your infinite possibilities. Or to put it another way, your self-worth is found in knowing who you are, in trying to see yourself the way God sees you. Your worth, as Coach Blitzer would say, is recognizing that you're "enough."

TO FIND YOURSELF, GET LOST!

Many people have accomplished great things or achieved great fame, and yet have felt empty and hollow. We even hear of movie and TV stars who destroy their lives with drugs, or wealthy people who commit suicide. What's up with that? They appear to "have it all," but something is missing. Perhaps they have not learned this great secret: The key to self-esteem is to take the focus off yourself and find a way to make a difference in the lives of others.

Let's take a close look at the word *self-esteem* for a minute. There are thousands of books at your local bookstore on the topic of "self-esteem." Listen to the words they use: *self-esteem, self-confidence, self-image, self-worth.* All these "self" words. (Santa and his elves use the words "elf-worth," "elf-confidence," and "elf-esteem." Ho, ho.) What do they all mean? It begins to sound kind of self-*ish*, doesn't it? If we're not careful, we might get so preoccupied with self-esteem that it becomes, well, self-centered.

Oddly enough, the secret to *finding* yourself is to *forget* yourself. It sounds backwards, but it's true.

An old Chinese proverb says it this way: "Help thy brother's boat across, and lo, thine own has reached the shore." And Ralph Waldo Emerson said, "It is one of the most beautiful compensations of this life that no man can sincerely try to help another without helping himself."

I'll bet all of us have had experiences of helping someone else and feeling wonderful about it. Have you ever done something for someone that you didn't have to do, or weren't being paid to do, but you did it anyway? Have you ever tried doing it anonymously? Well, how did it make you feel? See, it's true! You focus on others, and without even trying, your own worth comes into focus.

So, will knowing that your self-worth remains constant ensure that you will *always* feel good about yourself? Perhaps not. You'll still have ups and downs, and you'll still ride that roller coaster around. But as you get older and begin to understand life better, the roller coaster will even out quite a bit. The hills and valleys won't be as steep. Life will still bring its setbacks and trials and, unfortunately for some of us, even tragedies. That's what life is like. But your potential, your gifts, and your infinite possibilities to affect others for good remain unchanged.

Well, we're about done with this chapter, and I just have to ask, are you happy? Maybe a little happier than when we started? Well, we've still got a lot of reading to do, so don't give up on me yet. No matter how you esteem yourself right now, the rock-solid truth is that you have great worth, and your soul is precious. Stay away from the bad foundations of how others treat you, your appearance, or your accomplishments. Instead, build on the rock—your untapped potential, your infinite possibilities, and your unique gifts as a human being.

Your life is just getting started, my friend, so don't judge yourself by what you've done. Instead, look ahead and be (dare I say this word to teenagers? gulp . . .) patient! I believe that if you could look into the future and see what you have the potential to become, you would be astonished beyond all measure. It's going to take some work and some planning, but it's going to be a great ride, and you're gonna make it.

Join me next period for Persistence 101, and we'll look at the challenges of trying to discover your own unique gifts and potential. You know, I'm more impressed with you every minute. Not only did you start reading this book (which by itself shows that you are a remarkable teenager) but you just finished the second chapter!

Third Period
PERSISTENCE 101
Finding the prize inside

Nothing splendid has ever been achieved except by those who dared believe that something inside them was superior to circumstance.

—Bruce Barton

I believe that every one of us is like a box of Cracker Jacks. In fact, what you're about to hear is called the Cracker Jack theory. (Ooh, how intriguing!) If you're like me, when you get a box of Cracker Jacks, you try to open it at the end where the prize is. I usually get it wrong. Then I have to go through a lot of peanuts and popcorn before I find it.

In the same way, I believe that each one of us has a prize inside: something more wonderful than we can imagine right now, some great talent or ability or gift. Because of our impatience, we want to find the prize *right now*. We want to know *right now* what we can do and be. But some things in life are not so instant.

The library is full of stories of people who searched to find their prize. Albert Einstein once had trouble with math. Tom Cruise suffered with dyslexia. Michael Jordan was cut from his high school basketball team!

It may take a while for you to wade through all the peanuts and popcorn too, and that's what makes teenage life so interesting! But, and this is important, you have to keep believing that you have a prize inside. It's there. So keep chomping on the peanuts and popcorn until you get to the prize. Just remember that everyone who has become something in life has had to go through a lot of popcorn. Everyone! And you might too! But you are here for a reason. You have a destiny and a purpose. There *is* a prize inside of you.

I hope you'll forgive me if I use a few personal experiences here, but I have to use personal experiences about me because I don't know any personal experiences about you. When you write your book, then I'll read all about yours.

Anyway, I still remember my first day of high school. As soon as I stepped in the door, I recognized that I would have a few adjustments to make. The halls were so long, and there were so many classrooms, and the building seemed gigantic. Along with my cornet (oh yes, I had been a proud member of the eighth-grade band), I brought along many junior-high concerns. What if I couldn't make it from one end of the school to the other before the bell rang? What if I had to ask somebody how to find a room and they told me the wrong place on purpose? What if a senior locked me inside my locker? What if my lunch box wasn't cool? (Just kidding—I *knew* my lunch box was cool.) Everything was new and different. And some of the students! Wow, they were huge! They looked like . . . like . . . adults! There were big seniors who *shaved!* Some of the students drove cars to school! Incredible.

Another thing I began to notice was that some of

these students were really good at things. I heard seniors singing in the music rooms, and they had that wavy thing in their voice we call "vibrato." I saw student athletes in track, football, and basketball who were strong and skilled and talented. I saw drawings in the showcase done by some of the art students, and they were excellent. I saw nice-looking furniture on display that some other students had made in wood shop.

Seeing all these achievements made me wonder: *What can I do? What can I be?* Like lots of ninth graders, I didn't feel like I could do anything. I mean, I could do lots of things, but I wasn't really good at anything. I wanted to be good at something! Back in eighth grade, I had known a student named Joe. He seemed to be a fairly average kid. One day someone told me he was the number-four tennis player for his age group in the surrounding eight states. I looked at him differently after that; wouldn't you? I think when we find out that somebody does something really well, our respect for them increases. And I think our own self-respect may increase when we work at a talent or a hobby.

It's really nice to have something you can do well, something to give you satisfaction. In fact, I'd like to recommend to you that you find something you're good at, and work hard at it. (TV watching doesn't count.)

How about it? What can you do? Any ideas? I bet we could find things you could do for every letter of the alphabet. Ready? How about: archery, basketball, composing, drawing, exercise, football, golf, hiking, ice skating, jogging, kick soccer, listening, mowing, needlepoint, observing, piano playing, quilting, reading, singing, track and field, understanding, visiting, writing, xylophone, yodeling, and zoo! Okay, so some of them are a little lame, and some don't end in -ing, but you get the point.

Marvin J. Ashton has written: "One of the great tragedies of life, it seems to me, is when a person classifies himself as someone who has no talents or gifts. When, in disgust or discouragement, we allow ourselves to reach depressive levels of despair because of our demeaning self-appraisal, it is a sad day for us and a sad day in the eyes of God. For us to conclude that we have no gifts when we judge ourselves by our stature, intelligence, grade-point average, wealth, power, position, or external appearance is not only unfair but unreasonable. . . . It is up to each of us to search for and build upon the gifts which God has given" (*Ensign,* November 1987, p. 20).

If you feel that you have few talents or gifts, please remember that you are very young, and you've still got some peanuts and popcorn to go through. Many of us will try many different things, and even fail at many different things, before we find something we really love. But all of us have the capacity to do something right now. Let's go back to our alphabetical list for a second, and let's focus on "L" and "U"—listening and understanding. Folks, we have a shortage in this area. Our world needs more people who are good at those things. If you're at a loss for what you can be, then "listen" and "understand" this story from one mother:

> When my daughter, Mary, was just a small
> child, she was asked to perform a talent for a

PTA contest. This is her experience exactly as she wrote it in her seven-year-old script:

"I was practicing the piano one day and it made me cry because it was bad. Then I decided to practice ballet, and it made me cry more—it was bad too. So then I decided to draw a picture because I knew I could do that good, but it was horrid. Of course it made me cry.

"Then my little three-year-old brother came up and I said, 'Duffy, what *can* I be? What can *I* be? I can't be a piano player or an artist or a ballet girl. What can I be?' He came up to me and whispered, 'You can be my sister.'"

In an important moment, those five simple words changed the perspective and comforted the heart of a very anxious child. Life became better right on the spot and, as always, tomorrow was a brighter day. (Patricia T. Holland, *On Earth as it is in Heaven,* Deseret Book, 1989, p. 3)

Making a difference in the world may begin by making a difference in our family. We need more teenagers who will say in their hearts, "I am a world-class, All-American, gold-medal, top-ten big brother [or big sister]." Now, I know that some of you are thinking, "Oh, great, I can be good at something that doesn't matter." Oooh, be careful what you say! (Loud thunder, blinding lightning, more rumbling thunder . . .) It *does* matter to be a good brother or sister! In fact, the day will come when you realize that the most important roles we have in life involve our relationships with our families! So believe me when I say, we need more listeners and understanders. You can be that right away, tonight! Then you can start working on some other things, too.

Well, back in ninth grade, I really wasn't sure what I could do. I'd been trying to play the cornet since the sixth grade, but I was beginning to lose interest (the same way I lost interest in the playing the piano—two things I really regret today). I didn't know what I could do.

INTERSECTIONS AND HAPPY ACCIDENTS

A few years ago I saw a poster that said, "In Michigan in 1898 there were only two automobiles: they collided." What luck. In the whole state there were only two cars, and they ran into each other. We call that an accident.

The most likely places for cars to run into other cars are called intersections. But some intersections are no accident. You will "collide" with a lot of other people throughout your life, and maybe your bumping into each other was meant to be.

On freshman orientation day at the high school, I attended an assembly where loud young men and hyper young women jumped up and down and yelled a lot. They were really gung ho about school spirit, and they wanted us to act that way too. After that, I went to the gym to register for my classes. A bunch of teachers were sitting at tables around the edge of the gym. If you wanted to be in someone's class, you'd take a little card from that teacher's table, and you'd hand in your seven cards when you were done. After getting the required courses, English and math and so on, I had one elective to choose, and I was really excited. I had been looking over several selections, but Architectural Drawing seemed the most interesting to me. When I asked for a card, the teacher said, "I'm sorry, I'm all full. Why don't you take Commercial Art instead?" Obedient little ninth grader that I was, I picked up a card for Commercial Art. I didn't realize it at the time, but this was a happy accident—a great intersection in my life. I'm so glad that teacher recommended another class instead of just saying that he was full. I had always liked to draw, but now I "collided" with a great art teacher who taught me and inspired me and, for the next four years, helped me find something that I could be.

If I could take a moment to give you some brotherly advice, I'd tell you to make friends not only with the students in your school or neighborhood but with the teachers and adults, too. They can help you with so many intersections. They can steer you in the right direction and warn you when it's time to put on the brakes. I'll never forget John Peay, one of my adult advisors at my church. He was also my friend. Every week he would ask us, "How's it going?" And he really wanted to know. Together we had many long talks. We talked about things that I was too embarrassed to talk about with my parents. He helped me with my feelings of insecurity; he counseled me about the girls I wanted to meet; he even took me fishing, where we talked about all kinds of things in between the big ones that got away.

Thank heaven for decent adult role models. I hope you'll take advantage of having friendly adults around.

Whether they come from your school, your church, or your neighborhood, they have something to offer you, and you, as a smart teenager, will recognize that. Someone once said that wise people learn from experience, but superwise people learn from others' experi-

ences. That's one reason adult friends can be such an asset: You can learn from their experiences. My adult friends were not telling me what to do, they were telling me how to do it, and how to be happy!

If you think there's a big generation gap, take an honest look and make sure it's not the one between your headphones. Get over yourself, and go make friends with your teachers and leaders. It may just be that they're there for a reason—to help you. Maybe they don't speak your language or listen to your music, but a brilliant teenager like yourself will realize that they might know some things you haven't yet learned! They might have some great advice on how to be happier and make wiser choices concerning your future.

Throughout my ninth-grade year, I watched a lot of people do things that I wanted to do. But I was kind of, well, timid. (I had been stomped on before for trying to leave "my group," and I didn't like it.) Life continued. My ninth-grade year came and went, and like most ninth graders, I still battled the feelings of not belonging, of wondering what I could be. And when I opened the yearbook at the end of my ninth-grade year, I turned to the spot you and I always turn to first—our own picture. I looked through dozens of pages highlighting all the extracurricular activities: the music, the drama, the sports, and the honor clubs. Among all the pages of photos of people who seemed to know what they could be, I finally found my single, solitary photo in the rather unexciting section titled "Freshmen."

It took me years to see how these difficult times I went through were actually good for me. One of the hardest things to say to a teenager, and one of the hardest things for a teenager to hear, is this little two-word phrase: "Be patient."

IF AT FIRST YOU DON'T SUCCEED, YOU'RE RUNNING ABOUT AVERAGE

A new year finally dawned, and in my tenth-grade quest to answer the question, "What can I be?" I signed up for the track team. I liked it. It was an individual sport, which meant it didn't attract the crowds like basketball and football, but I enjoyed being outside during the last period of the day, and I liked to run. I mean, when I first signed up I liked to run. It seemed like the goal of the track coaches was to make you hate to run. I quickly developed a case of shin splints, but I kept running. I ran each day until I was thoroughly spent. At the end of each workout I would go home and ask myself, *Why do I push myself to the brink of exhaustion every day? What is the point of all this?* But then I'd do it all again the next day.

One day I came home for lunch expecting to eat my usual preworkout meal: a small piece of toast and a glass of orange juice. But my sister, who had stayed home sick from school that day and didn't know my routine, had made me a huge bacon, lettuce, and tomato sandwich. I mean, what was I supposed to do? As soon as I walked in the door, she came walking toward me with her furry slippers and her "bed head" of messy hair, with this look-what-I-did-for-you-because-I'm-a-great-sister look on her face. Because I didn't want to make her feel bad, I ate it all. I went back to school feeling a little too full.

About an hour later, I was running laps. The coach  had the whole team run in a single file around the track at about 75 percent of sprint speed. The person who was in the front of the line had to run at a full sprint around the 440-yard track until he ran all the way around and caught up with the back of the line. Upon his arrival, he'd slow to 75 percent and yell "go," and the next person at the front of the line would take off at sprint speed. This continued until everyone in the line had a turn. Sounds fun, eh?

By the time I finished, I was sick. Really sick. I felt like I was going to lose my lunch. I was a virtual time-bomb of pork strips, red and green vegetables, and Wonder Bread waiting to explode. So I did something I had never done before. I asked the coach if I could leave the workout early. I went back to the locker room and took a shower. As I walked out of the locker room, finally it all came out. I won't use any gross slang, I'll just tell you I tossed that BLT all over an evergreen bush. I felt a lot better, and I went home and slept. (I didn't tell my sister what happened to the lunch she made me.)

The next week I walked out that same door and noticed that the bush was dead. I had discovered a new herbicide: one BLT and a track workout.

Track workouts were hard, but track meets were really fun. It was especially fun to watch the relays. I did my best that year, but I didn't have a lot of success. In the spring I attended the state qualifying meet at Skyline High School. I remember warming up for the second heat of the 220. I was assigned lane two. One by one, the other runners came to the starting line. When the runners took their spots, the announcer gave the names of those in each lane. "In lane one," he began, "Mike Matheson, senior, East High School." I turned my head and stared right into the kneecap of the 6'8" all-state basketball player. *Oh, joy,* I thought, as all 5'10" of me settled into the blocks. "Lane two, John . . . Bith, uh, Byth-way." After the rest of the introductions, I placed my feet into the starting blocks and waited. After some anxious anticipation, the starting gun fired, and I exploded out of the blocks! I had stayed after workouts and practiced my starts on more than one occasion—I was quick. I couldn't see anyone on either side of me, until the legs belonging to that 6'8" speed machine next to me began to stride out, and I watched him pass me in lane one. I lengthened my stride, I quickened my pace, and I ran the fastest time I'd ever run in the 220 that day. But I didn't come in first. And I didn't come in second, and I didn't come in third, and I didn't come in fourth. I wasn't fifth or sixth, and I wasn't seventh. I came in eighth. There were eight runners in that heat. As I crossed the finished line, put my hands on my hips, and slowed to a walk with my head down, I heard a little voice in the back of my head make a brilliant observation: "John, maybe track isn't your thing."

Later in the year, I got my grade for track: C + . I was not a happy camper. I shed some of my timidity and stormed into the coach's office. "Coach," I began, "I've been to every workout, I've worked my tail off, I haven't been a slacker. The only workout I ever missed was because I was sick, and I have the dead bush to prove it. I'm not the fastest runner, but I have done everything you've asked, and I think I deserve an A." Thankfully, he changed my grade, and I got an A in track.

But more important than that A were some other voices I heard at that state qualifying meet. Although I had been soundly defeated that day, three of the seniors on my track team spoke to me: "Nice job, Bytheway," "Hey, nice try," "Good effort, Bytheway." They had seen me at the workouts. They knew I worked hard. I suppose that, although I was still slower than molasses, I had earned a little bit of respect for trying.

Now, you may be wondering why I told you this story. First of all, I thought it was funny (at least the part about the BLT and the bush). But the main reason was to let you know that we all struggle to find the prize inside. We all struggle to find out what we can do and what we can be. Don't get discouraged if you don't succeed at everything you try! I didn't get a medal, and I didn't get to compete in the state finals, which means I didn't get a varsity letter. In fact, the only "lettering" I did in high school was making signs in Commercial Art class. But I'm really glad I ran track. I learned how hard I could push myself, and I learned a little bit more about what I enjoyed, what I didn't enjoy, and what I wanted to be. Marvin J. Ashton said, "True happiness is not made in getting something. True happiness is becoming something." Every experience, every setback, and every loss helps you to become a better person if you choose to handle it that way.

As my junior year approached, I knew I would have to take some risks, and I had some choices to make. Should I run track again, or should I get involved in music? Both took place during seventh period, so I had to choose one or the other. Judging from my past performance in track, I decided to try out for the Junior Choir. This meant I had to sing, by myself, in front of the teacher and many other people. But, I thought, what was the worst thing that could happen? I'd get nervous, goof up, and not get in the choir. Big deal!

I have found that this question can be very therapeutic. When you're faced with something that makes you nervous, just ask yourself, "What's the worst that could happen?" Usually, the answer is not that bad. The word *fear* can be thought of as standing for "False Expectations Appearing Real," and sometimes, false expectations make the consequences of failure seem bigger than they really are. If I didn't get into Junior Choir, hey, I'd run track again and kill a few more bushes with my homemade herbicide. No biggie. The point? If you and I are ever going to move forward, we've got to face the possibility of failure, and we've got to take some risks.

Risks

To laugh is—to risk appearing the fool.

To weep is—to risk appearing sentimental.

To reach out for another is—to risk involvement.

To expose your feelings is—to risk exposing your true self.

To place your ideas, your dreams, before the crowd is—to risk their loss.

To love is—to risk not being loved in return.

To live is—to risk dying.

To hope is—to risk despair.

To try is—to risk failure.

But risks must be taken, because the greatest hazard in life is to risk nothing. The person who risks nothing, does nothing, has nothing, and is nothing. He may avoid suffering and sorrow, but he simply cannot learn, feel, change, grow, love—live. Chained by his certitudes, he is a slave, he has forfeited freedom.

Only a person who risks is free. (From the *President's Newsletter*, Phi Beta Kappa, November 1982)

Everything we do involves risk. It's risky to get up in the morning; it's risky to walk across the street; heck, these days, it's risky to breathe! Well, welcome to life! If you can't stand the heat, get out of the kitchen! A ship is safe in the harbor, but that's not what ships are built for! Let's see, can I come up with any other clichés? No, but here's a great statement by Les Brown: "Life is like a game, and no one gets out alive: You can either die on the bleachers, or you can die on the field." As a junior, I decided I was sick of watching the game from the stands.

As you get out there on the playing field, I think you'll find that you learn a lot more from your failures than from your successes. Successes are easy to handle. But you always grow the most from the tough times. The supreme reward of struggle is strength!

Well, the time for my tryout came. I showed up in the music room at the appointed time with several other people. I sang "America the Beautiful" a capella style, and I'm sure it wasn't that beautiful (my singing, that is). But lo and behold, I made it into the choir. It wasn't as hard or as horrible as I had thought. I enjoyed the class, I enjoyed the music, and I became friends with a lot of great people. And I felt pretty stupid for having worried about it so much.

One day we were singing a song called "Up, Up and Away," and our teacher, "Mr. C," mentioned that it would be nice to have someone play the drums to accompany the song. After class, I asked Mr. C if I could play the drums. I had a really cheap drum set at home and, although I had never had drum lessons, I thought I could do it. He told me to bring my sticks, and he would give me a try. I looked forward to it with a healthy dose of fear . . . I mean, uh, faith. Seventh period finally arrived, and we started to rehearse. Eventually, Mr. C asked me to come down and sit at the drum set. So I took my seat on the little drum stool and faced the whole choir. I didn't have any drum music, I just told Mr. C I knew the song and could do it.

As I adjusted my chair, I thought to myself, *This is your chance. Don't be nervous, or you'll mess up.* I watched Mr. C for the tempo, "1–2–3–4," and we were under way. I laid into those drums with everything I had. My right hand was hitting eighth notes on the high-hat, my left hand was striking the snare, and my right foot was pounding the bass drum. I felt like "Animal" on *The Muppet Show*—arms and legs flying everywhere and lots of noise. The drums were loud, and the choir was belting it out, and I thought it sounded great. I was in my own world, crashing cymbals and wailing on drums, when suddenly I noticed that the choir had stopped. So I stopped. Nobody was saying a word. With the sound of the cymbals still ringing, I looked up at the choir, and they were all smiling. Then I looked at Mr. C, and he was looking at me with an expression of surprise and a slight grin. The whole room was silent. Finally I said, "Was that okay?" He answered with a smile, "Oh yeah, it was fine; it was just too loud!" The whole class erupted with laughter. I blushed several shades of red, and then I laughed too. That night I wrote in my journal, "Something I doubted would ever happen happened today. I found myself playing the drums while the Junior Choir sang 'Up, Up and Away.' I doubted that I would ever get a drum set, let alone that I would be accompanying a high school group." Fortunately, a little faith and effort overcame those doubts. Later in the year, the Junior Choir gave a concert, and I got to accompany them on the drums (I played a little softer this time).

So, what can you be? Anything you want to. But take your time. You don't have to find the prize and figure out life by Tuesday. Don't worry. It will come. Keep looking and trying and risking new things, and somewhere between the popcorn and peanuts, you'll stumble onto something that you love. Keep munching, but keep smiling. (Try to chew with your mouth closed, though, and be sure to check for food particles clinging to the outside of your face before you go back to class.)

Thanks for listening! Go get something to eat (a *real* box of Cracker Jacks springs to mind), and I'll see you in Fourth Period.

Fourth Period

DISCIPLINE 101

What my braces taught me about life

*Don't let life discourage you;
everyone who got where he is
had to begin where he was.*

—*Richard L. Evans*

G o look in the mirror and smile. What do you see? Food particles? A little speck of pepper? Maybe some Cracker Jacks? Well, go get a toothpick. Now look again. Is there an arrangement of wire, metal, and rubber bands? Maybe you don't need braces, but if you do have them, you carry a lesson about life right there in your mouth.

What do we know about braces? They hurt. They're ugly. They get food stuck in them. They're with you every second of the day. They make it harder to brush your teeth. People call you "brace face," "tin grin," and "metal molars" when you walk down the halls.

If braces are such a pain, why do we wear them? Duh! (This was a rhetorical question.) To straighten our teeth! You're going to feel the pain now so you can have a killer smile later! Sometimes it can take several years to get the job done, but when those braces come off, it is the greatest feeling. You look in the mirror, you smile, you run your tongue across the front of your teeth. All day at school, you look for chances to grin and laugh so that everyone can see your perfect, straight teeth. You eat caramel apples and corn on the cob. It's a day you'll never forget.

When I got my braces, I watched my orthodontist carefully. I mean, what else can you do? It's quite a comfortable chair, but you can only stare at the pattern of the ceiling tiles for so long, and I had already given up trying to impress the cute hygienist. Sitting there with your mouth open as wide as possible and all your various throat parts in full view is not very attractive, especially when they keep sticking that mini vacuum-thing in there—it makes such a nice sound, doesn't it? After I got home and swallowed a couple of Advils, I looked in the mirror and inspected the inside of my mouth until I had the "theory of braces" all figured out. Now, I'd like to give you this oral report.

This is how braces work: It's a cooperative effort between a wire, brackets, and rubber bands. If you have braces, it's because your teeth are crooked. And since teeth are a little hard to grab on to, the people at the orthodontist's office glue a bracket to the front of each tooth. Then, they form a paper-clip-size wire into the shape they want your teeth to be in, and they attach the wire to your teeth with rubber bands. And what do the rubber bands do? Well, besides coming in several neon and decorative colors to match each holiday, *they pull your teeth to the wire.* The wire is where your teeth *ought* to be. The rubber bands pull them there. Get it?

It takes a lot of pulling, and for the first few days after each adjustment, you can eat only manly meals like yogurt and soup. After many adjustments over the months and years, the teeth settle into their new position, and with the help of a retainer, they stay. Aah, victory at last! Braces hurt. And they're a pain. They're ugly, too. But they do great things for your mouth.

BRACE YOURSELF!

So what am I getting at in this chapter? Brace yourself. Say it slowly—Brace your *self!* In life, like in your mouth, if you want to get to a certain place, it might take some time, and it might take some pain. But it's all worth it in the end, because it's where you really want to be. So here's the lesson, straight from your mouth:

Crooked teeth = Where you are now
The wire = Where you want to be
Rubber bands = How you're gonna get there

Let me give you an example of a "wire," or a place you want your life to be. Let's say you want to graduate from high school with a certain grade-point average— that's the wire. How do you get there? You pull yourself there with gigantic rubber bands! The rubber bands are called studying and self-control. It's a pain! But when you graduate, it will feel great, and you'll keep that accomplishment for the rest of your life.

It all has to do with the strange relationship between discipline and freedom. What do discipline and freedom have in common? You might say, "Not much." But think about it. The fact is, one leads to the other. For example, what if every time you say, "Let's study for biology tonight," your friend says, "No way. I hate studying. I want to do what I want. I want my freedom." Months later, what happens when you get an "A" in biology, and your friend has to take the class over again? Who has more freedom then? Aha, neener, neener, right?

You may be thinking, "I know, but I hate studying. Discipline is a pain." Exactly! It is. But hey, welcome to life. "Life is pain, Highness," said the Dread Pirate Roberts whose name was really Wesley. (Remember *The Princess Bride?*) Someone else once said, "There are two kinds of pain in life: the pain of discipline, and the pain of regret. Discipline weighs ounces, but regret weighs tons." So you get to choose which kind of pain you want most. Why does discipline weigh only ounces? Because a little discipline, a little at a time, goes a long way over a long time.

In life, sometimes you have to do what you don't want to do in order to get what you want to get. You want a beautiful smile? Fine, but it's going to take a few years of pain. It is worth it? Ask anyone who has gone through the braces experience.

Every day we have many opportunities to choose between what feels good now and what feels not so good now, but will get us where we want to go. Sometimes being disciplined means feeling not so good now, so you can feel much better in the future. Please see Highly Informative Chart #1 on the next page for some examples:

Highly Informative Chart #1

Feels Good Now:	*Feels Not So Good Now:*
Veg in front of the television	Study and improve your mind
Stuff yourself with Twinkies and pop	Eat what gives you energy and strength
Sleep in and mope all day	Get up and early and work on your goals
Do less than expected at your job	Do more than expected at your job
Stay up late, sleep in	"Early to bed, early to rise"
Relax and don't move much	Exercise
The more you do this, the worse you get	The more you do this, the better you get
This leads to dependence, bondage	This leads to responsibility, freedom
Do this, and you could end up in the state pen	Do this, and you could end up at Penn State

I know there are some athletes out there reading this book, and you know all about this stuff. Almost every high school weight room I've ever seen has a sign in it that says, "It takes pain to gain." The conditioning, the weight lifting, the exercising, the workouts—they all have a purpose: to cause physical pain and mental torture. Actually, their purpose is to bring you to top physical condition! All those football, basketball, and baseball stars you see making things look easy on the highlight films at night didn't get there by vegging on television and snarfing junk food. They worked hard. They did what didn't feel good in the short run so that they could achieve something better in the long run.

The same is true of people who have reached high degrees of skill in any area. You've probably heard the story of the man who approached the concert pianist and said, "I would give my life to be able to play like that," and the concert pianist answered, "I did."

IT ALL COMES DOWN TO THE WIRE

The secret to enduring the braces on your teeth is this: Focus on the final result. When your teeth move to the wire, the braces come off. The secret to enduring life is the same thing: *Focus on what you're trying to become.* In other words, it all comes down to the wire. The question is, where do you want to be? Or, in other words, where are your wires?

I have a friend named Greg. I heard him give a speech to teenagers in which he shared his amazing personal story of becoming what he wanted to be. I should start by saying that Greg looks like one of those guys on the cover of a J. Crew catalog. No exaggeration. The girls all say he's "gorgeous," which makes the story even more interesting.

Greg told of a time back in his early high school years when he had no friends and was very overweight. He didn't feel all that good about himself, and he just kind of moved along through life like everyone else. One day something interesting happened. There was a popular girl at his school who walked up to Greg and simply said, "Greg, are you everything you want to be?" Deep inside, Greg answered to himself, "No." He knew he could be better.

This simple question from a wise young woman served as a wake-up call for Greg. He knew he was more than he was demonstrating. He determined where he wanted his "wire," and all that summer, he worked. He exercised like crazy and lost a lot of weight. He changed his diet and built up some muscle by working out. When Greg went back to school in the fall, he looked totally different. Nobody recognized him! They thought he was a new kid who had just moved in. He made a lot of friends and soon became one of the most popular guys at the school.

Greg humbly explained that he got kind of caught up in his newfound popularity. After a while, unfortunately, he wasn't treating people as well as he should have. Once again, this girl came to Greg and asked the same question: "Greg, are you everything you want to be?" And once again, Greg answered, "No." He looked deep inside. He had already changed his appearance, but perhaps there was more remodeling to be done. Now he had to form a new wire for his heart. He decided he would talk to everyone, not just those in the popular group, and he would start treating everyone with respect and kindness and class. And he did!

I really love this story. It happened because a friend kept asking that wonderful question, "Are you everything you want to be?" and because Greg was willing to answer the question, form a wire, and pull himself to his new standard.

As a teenager, I was always intrigued with the idea of being "classy." I'm not very sure how to define *class,* but I think you already know what it is. There were many different sorts of people at my high school: some were loud, some were quiet, some were outgoing, some were shy, some were obnoxious, some were mean, some were gross, and some were brilliant. As I looked around, it seems I was always drawn to the people who had "class." They seemed to have a quiet kind of self-assurance. They weren't showy or loud. They didn't cut people down to make themselves feel superior. They had a quiet confidence that was impressive.

I wanted that same trait for myself. So I observed. Observation means keeping your mouth shut and your eyes and ears open, and it's one of the smartest things you can do. I watched, I listened, I observed. I found people I deeply respected, people whom I really wanted to be like, and I studied them. I asked myself, "How do they talk? What do they talk about? What do they laugh at? What do they walk away from? How do they dress? How do they treat people who can't do them any good?" When I felt like I had a handle on these things, I tried to develop those traits in myself.

There are so many different wires in your life that it would take another book to describe them all. Let's just narrow it down to a few broad categories:

Social wires. The last few examples elaborated on how you can improve yourself socially. Find the traits you admire in others, write them down, and then focus on developing them in your own life. A *Wall Street Journal* article recently reported that the number-one reason business managers fail is their inability to get along with others. It didn't mention anything about grades or test scores! I believe that this is true not just of business managers but of everyone.

High school is a great time to learn and develop

social skills. As with all areas of your life, be patient with yourself on this one. Remember that your high school experience is not a forecast for your life.

Career and financial wires. It may seem strange to talk about careers and money-smarts in a book for teenagers. However, as you will see in a chapter soon to come, starting while you're young on some of these principles can make a huge difference to your future. Wait until Fifth Period and we'll talk about this in a lot more detail.

Spiritual wires. Because of the amazing number of different beliefs in our country, and because of the intensely personal nature of spirituality, I have to approach this topic carefully. But almost everybody acknowledges a spiritual side to his or her life. In fact, one study that I read revealed that 96 percent of Americans believe in God, and 92 percent say they pray once a week!

With all the television and newspaper coverage, you might think that sports are more popular than religion. If so, here's another interesting statistic: A 1996 study found that more people attend worship services on any one weekend than attend all the Major League Baseball, National Basketball Association, and National Football League games throughout the entire year! More than 105 million people on a typical weekend are in a church, synagogue, or mosque. (See Zig Ziglar, *Over the Top,* Thomas Nelson Publishers, 1997, p. 239.) Clearly, spirituality is a vital part of life for many people.

The spiritual realm is important because it attempts to answer the questions, "Where did I come from?"

"Why am I here?" and "Where am I going after I die?" If you find peace and purpose in your spiritual life, clearly this would be another area in which to set goals. These goals might include setting aside time for study, devotion, and service to others.

Physical wires. Everyone understands the phrase, "You are what you eat." We ought to eat the things that cleanse and energize our bodies rather than the things that clog and pollute. In addition to the foods you eat, you have to make a decision about whether or not to use drugs, alcohol, or tobacco. But that choice is such a no-brainer that I'm not even going to mention it further.

We also understand that exercise does amazing things for our physical and mental health. Since our bodies are the things that carry around our eyes, ears, mouths, and brains, we ought to try to maintain them so that they will last a long time. In college I took a class

called "Fitness for Life." On the first day, our professor promised us that if we would exercise for a half an hour at a time, three to four times a week, we would see our studying improve, we would fall asleep faster, we wouldn't need to sleep as long, and we would be so thrilled with the results that we wouldn't ever want to stop.

Oh boy, was he right. In order to get an A, we had to run about a mile and a half in under eleven minutes, which meant we all had to train by jogging three to four times a week. Well, I trained, and in the final run got my A, but in the weeks that followed, I found I couldn't stop running. Even though the class was over, I couldn't sit still in the evenings. I had to put on my running shoes and take off again. It wasn't the actual running that I enjoyed so much as the feeling that would come an hour or so after I was done. I think they call it "runner's high." Exercising is a classic example of doing what feels not so good now so that you can live longer and feel great later.

Intellectual wires. You and I are in the middle of a booming information age. In fact, there is so much information out there that we have to be choosy about what we read, watch, and listen to so that it will move us where we want to go. You are already in good shape because you are reading a book. I hope you think it's a good book. Many people, once they graduate from high school or college, never pick up another book. From then on, it's TV land every night for the rest of their lives. What a pathetic waste.

I have turned my car into a classroom on wheels. Wherever I go, I carry a bunch of tapes. Music tapes? No (although I love music). They are books on tape and seminars on tape, and I love 'em. You can learn a language, listen to the classics, or get caught up in a great novel while you drive. I can't tell you how many exits I've missed because I was thoroughly engrossed in the book I was listening to. (Where do you think most of the quotes I've used in this book come from?)

If you think that sounds boring, think of the alternative. When you're on a long road trip, you could listen to book after book and become wiser with every mile, or you could fill your head with the vocabulary of an R-rated disc jockey, or become thoroughly depressed about the shape the country's in while listening to talk radio. Which do you think will best help you reach your goals, hmmm?

SMILE! THE BEST IS YET TO COME

To me, one of the most exciting things I've discovered is that I can shape my own life by deciding what I want to be and then pulling myself toward that ideal with goals. A long time ago, a psychologist named William James said, "The greatest discovery of my generation is that a human being can alter his life by altering his attitudes of mind." You can totally change your life too. Instead of throwing up your hands and saying, "This is just the way I am," take some time to be alone, plan out the person you want to be, and become what you plan. George Bernard Shaw once said, "Some men see things as they are, and say, 'Why?' I dream of things that never were and say, 'Why not?'"

Some people feel like they are completely shaped by their past. Maybe they came from a broken home or the wrong side of town, or they didn't have the right opportunities or money, or maybe they blame it on the fact that they're a Virgo, or whatever. The fact is, you are not your past. Did you get that? *You are not your past!* Whatever your past is, your future is still undetermined. And PUH-LEASE, don't think your life is controlled by big burning balls of gas billions of miles away (astrology). I'm not even going there. And I'm not going to the "Psychic Hotline," either. Rise above all that "for entertainment only" baloney, and take control of your life!

You can do it! Thomas A. Edison once said, "If we did all the things we are capable of doing, we would literally astound ourselves." May you spend most of your life being astounded, my friend.

Life can be a pain, but it can also be incredibly fun. If some things feel crooked in your life, brace yourself! Don't worry about the things you can't control, but take charge of the things you can. Just remember, it all comes down to the wire!

Fifth Period

PERSONAL FINANCE 101

Get a job!

> *My grandfather once told me that there are two kinds of people: those who do the work and those who take the credit. He told me to try to be in the first group; there was much less competition there.*
>
> *—Indira Gandhi*

During my high school years, I had several jobs. I worked mowing lawns, I worked doing odd jobs for a contractor, and I worked in the basement of a department store. Yes, *prestige* was my middle name.

It's nice to have a job. It's nice to have some "extra money" (if there is such a thing), and it's nice to learn some responsibility. I only wish I had known then what I know now. And I, your devoted author, in a fearless search for all the things I wish I'd known in high school, have wielded my mighty machete in the jungle of knowledge and uncovered another nugget of treasure lying beneath the thick overgrowth (being careful at all times, of course, not to damage the rain forest).

HOW TO GET A JOB

So, you want to make some extra money, and you saw the "help wanted" sign at Honkin' Burger, the local fast food drive-in. You've picked up an application, and now you're ready for your interview. How do you prepare? Good question.

Your main goal is to get a job, so you'd better try to  be as impressive as possible. There are entire books written about how to have a good job interview, but for our purposes, may I just mention a few basics? First, dress up. I know the trend these days is to dress down, but don't. Dress up. Look impressive, look sharp.

I know a young man who had trouble finding a job because he had a pierced tongue. His attitude was, "Well, if they don't like it, that's their problem." Yeah, he sure showed them. But guess who still doesn't have a job?

Your new employer may have a dress code, and he or she will be wondering how you'll respond to it. My advice is, give yourself every chance to succeed, even if that means giving up the latest fad.

The person who will interview you is going to wonder how you'll come across to customers, so do the basic hygiene thing. (Do I really have to mention this?) Wash your hair, brush your teeth, shave, use deodorant! If you're concerned about your appearance in the interview, they'll know that you'll be concerned when you don their stunning two-tone polyester Honkin' Burger uniform and begin serving customers.

Next, when you come to the interview, stand up straight, shake hands, look the interviewer in the eye, and smile. Don't look at the floor and mumble (unless you see a roach). If you feel like you don't have the self-confidence you want, just act as if you did.

The interviewer may ask you a million different questions, but there's one almost every interviewer will ask, and that's this: "Why should I hire you?"

Bad answers to this question would include, "'Cause I need the money," "My dad says I should get a job because I'm always getting in trouble," or the ever-popular, "I don't know." A good answer might be, "Because I will be a great employee. You'll never have to worry about me being late, I know how to get along with others, I'm a fast learner, and I will be concerned about keeping our customers happy." (Calling them "our customers" instead of "your customers" is a nice touch.) Of course, if you get hired, you have to keep your word and do all those things. The thing you want the interviewer to be thinking is, "Wow, this kid is incredible! I would be a fool not to hire him/her! This kid must read John Bytheway books!" (Yeah, like they would really say that.)

Another very tricky question interviewers often ask is, "What is your worst trait?" Oooh, sinister and clever. What do you say? I got this question once, and I started to squirm in my chair. I finally came up with, "Well, I like to have fun, and I love to laugh. But while I'm at work, I'll focus on my job and make that trait an asset and not a liability." Try to answer that question in a positive way, and let them know that your weaknesses won't become their problem. You wouldn't want to say anything like, "Well, I tend to burn down things and destroy property," or, "You know, my warden used to say . . ." I mean, try to tell the truth, but let them know you are working on your weaknesses.

The last thing most interviewers will say is, "Do you have any questions for me?" The best answer to this is, "Yes." I think interviewers are impressed when you have things that you want to know. Be careful what you ask, however. You probably would not want to start out with, "So, how easy is it to get days off work?" But there are lots of other things you could ask. If you haven't already discussed it, you could ask about the wage you'll be earning. (If it's minimum wage, don't worry. That's where everybody starts. We'll talk about how to get a raise later.) You might ask about opportunities for advancement. You might ask what incentive programs are offered by Honkin' Burger. I think most interviewers are impressed when you become the interviewer and ask, "Is this really where *I* want to work?"

Hopefully, they'll hire you on the spot. If not, when the interview is over, stand up, shake hands, and thank them for the interview. They'll probably say, "We have some other interviews to conduct, so we'll let you know in a few days." So here's what you do: go home and write a thank-you note expressing gratitude for the interview. End the letter with, "I'll look forward to hearing from you." After you send the letter, remember three basic rules: Follow up, follow up, and, number three, follow up. The day after your thank-you note arrives, you might make a phone call and say, "I hope I'm not bothering you, I was just wondering if you had any news for me yet." Be polite, but keep following up. Remember the old saying, "The squeaky wheel gets the grease" (which seems appropriate when thinking of fast food).

If you don't get hired, don't get discouraged. You'll find another job, maybe with even better polyester uniforms. Politely ask the interviewer if there's anything you could have done differently to get the job. The person may be able to give you some good advice.

I'm not really too worried about you getting a job. I think any teenager who is interested in reading books and has already reached the fifth chapter of this one is an exceptional person. I think you'll be fine. If you want more information on getting a job, see the counseling center at your high school. In addition to giving you interviewing tips, they can alert you to many legal issues involved with interviewing and hiring that you may want to be aware of. Bottom line: Be at your best, look your best, and behave your best.

HOW TO GET A RAISE

After I graduated from high school, I did some volunteer work for my church in the Philippines. It was fantastic. My boss was a very successful businessman, and I got to work with him side by side for seven months. Quite a rare opportunity for a nineteen-year-old!

I was in a supervisory position, and several times a day, I would go into his office and say, "Excuse me, but there's a problem down in this area, and uh, what should we do?" At first, he'd tell me what to do and I'd leave. About an hour later, I'd be in his office again, bringing up problems and asking for solutions. One day he said to me, "John, sit down for a minute. Do you want to know how to get ahead in business?" I nodded. What he said next was only four words long, but it proved to be some of the best common-sense business advice I have ever heard. He looked me in the eye and said, "Solve your boss's problems."

I had been going about it all wrong. I thought that you were supposed to go to the boss with every problem because he was, well, the boss! But my boss, Menlo Smith, had a different philosophy. He always used to say, "A good leader trains leaders while he leads." He continued, "I don't ever want you to come in here again with a dilemma unless you have a solution. I'm not interested in your problems, I'm interested in your rec-ommendations." Then he gave me what he called "The Five Levels of Delegation." Here they are:

1. Seek problems, solve them, keep it to yourself.

2. Seek problems, solve them, report back what you did.

3. Seek problems, recommend a solution to your boss.

4. Seek problems, come to the boss, and say, "What should we do?"

5. Wait till the boss finds out about a problem and comes to you.

He said, "John, we're going to work on level three, okay? You stay in your office until you think you have the best solution in mind, and during our daily planning meeting, you can tell me what you think we ought to do. If you get really good at this, I'll move you to level two. How does that sound?"

Well, I wrote it all down, and that's why I still

remember it. It forced me to think. Sometimes, when thinking over a problem, I would sit in my office and say, "What would Menlo Smith do about this?" The amazing thing is, when I just switched gears a little bit and thought of myself as a problem *solver* instead of a problem *reporter,* I could usually figure out what he would do. Within a few weeks, I'm happy to report, I was allowed to move to level two. Imagine how I felt! He trusted me! And, eventually, I hit the big time. Yes, I played the palace. I worked at level one. In fact, one time my boss went to Singapore for two weeks and I had to run the whole show. I was twenty years old at the time. Do you want to get ahead in business? *Solve your boss's problems.*

Now, if you're working at our hypothetical Honkin' Burger, don't just assume you should start at level one. You'll need to earn your boss's trust first. I would start at level two or three. You'll impress your boss right off if you walk in the back office one day and say, "Mr. Jones, while you were gone we ran out of sesame seed buns for our "Sesame Seed Combo Honkin' Surprise" meal. I told everybody to use the regular ones and explain to the customers that we were out of our sesame buns. I also left a note on your desk telling you what I did, and took a quick inventory of how many regular buns we have left." Do you think your boss will be impressed? More impressed than if you just said, "Mr. Jones, we ran out of sesame buns, uh, what should we do?" Just remember your boss has plenty of other problems to solve, many of which you don't even know about. Imagine how refreshing it would be to have an employee who knows how to solve problems and make decisions on his or her own!

Here's another example of an employee thinking on his feet. I heard this story on one of those tapes I listen to while I drive:

> When Andrew Carnegie was a young clerk for the Pennsylvania Railroad in Pittsburgh, he came to the office one morning and discovered that there had been a bad train wreck just outside the city. He tried desperately to reach the superintendent by telephone but was unable to do so. Finally, in desperation, he did something that he knew could mean his automatic discharge because of the company's strict rules. Recognizing that every minute of delay was costing the railroad a fortune, he wired instructions to the conductor, signing the boss's name.
>
> When the superintendent came to his desk several hours later, he found Carnegie's resignation and an explanation of what he had done. The day passed, and nothing happened. Several days later, his boss called Carnegie into his office and said, "Young man, there are two kinds of people who never get ahead. One is the fellow who will not do what he is told, and the other is the fellow who will not do anything more than he is told." In this instance, the boss found Carnegie more valuable than the railroad's policies. (Napoleon Hill, *Napoleon Hill's A Year of Growing Rich*, Penguin Highbridge Audio, 1993)

It was a gutsy move, but Carnegie studied the situation out in his mind and solved his boss's problem.

So, how do you get a raise? Well, there are a lot of things you could do. An average employee will do what's expected, but you can do more than expected. The average employee will be a minute or two late, but you can be a minute or two early. The average employee will complain about conditions, but you will say, "What can I do to make conditions better?" As Og Mandino has written:

> You need not love the tasks you do. Even kings dream of other occupations. Yet you must work, and it is how you do, not what you do, that determines the course of your life. No man who is careless with a hammer will ever build a palace.
>
> You may work grudgingly or you may work gratefully; you may work as a human or you may work as an animal. Still, there is no work so rude that you may not exalt it; no work so demeaning that you cannot breathe a soul into it; no work so dull that you may not enliven it. Always perform all that is asked of you and more. Thy reward will come. (*The Greatest Success in the World*, Bantam Books, 1981, p. 66)

Above all, be willing to learn. Ask a lot of questions. The more you know about what you're doing, the more valuable you'll become to your boss. Remember the old saying, "Catch me a fish and I eat for a day; teach me to fish, and I eat for a lifetime." If you ask a lot of questions, you'll be "learning to fish." And that knowledge will stay in your head for whatever jobs you have for the rest of your life.

HOW TO GET SOME FINANCIAL INDEPENDENCE

What I'd like to do next is get you interested in interest. Interested? Good. I'll try to make it interesting.

I took an accounting class in college called "The Time Value of Money." Before then, I knew a little bit about interest, but I wasn't really that, um, interested. What I learned in class blew me away. My main thought was, "Why didn't someone tell me this sooner?" That's why I'm telling you now!

Simply put, interest is what a bank pays you to save your money in one of their accounts. If you put $100 in an account, and they pay you 5 percent interest ("compounded" or calculated annually), in one year you'll have $105. The next year, they'll give you 5 percent of $105, which is $5.25, giving you a total of $110.25. See how it works? You made interest on your interest.

Now let's try a more "interesting" example: Let's say you're fifteen years old. What would happen if you saved $50 a month every month until you were sixty-five? That doesn't sound too hard, does it? Let's say you had a savings account that paid 5 percent interest compounded monthly. What you would actually put into the account over fifty years would be $30,000. But what you would earn in interest is $103,425.64, giving you a total of $133,425.64!

What if you spend all you earn now, and wait until you're twenty-five years old to start saving $50 a month? Then your total balance at age sixty-five is only $41,610.81. When I heard this in my college class, I realized that those extra ten years of not saving my money cost me $91,814.83! So what's the point? START NOW! If you can get on a regular savings program *now,* you'll be making interest on your interest, and that's the "time value of money." You'll be doing what most teenagers, and sadly, most supposedly educated adults are not doing.

It's absolutely stupefying to me that people don't or won't save their money. As Dennis R. Deaton, author of *Money: An Owner's Manual,* wisely observed, "There are only two laws that have to be applied in order to accumulate money:

"Law No. 1: Don't Spend All You Earn.

"Law No. 2: Don't Lose What You Save."

These laws are simple, but they're not easy to follow. There are a million people (salespeople and retailers) who think you *should* spend all you earn, and you *should* borrow beyond what you earn, so they can get *interest* out of you! They want you making payments to them! This is the opposite side of interest. When you get a loan, you "rent" the money from the bank, and the rent you pay is a percentage of what you owe. Get it? The problem is, what you owe grows bigger every second of every day!

Let's say you get a five-year loan for $5,000 at 10

percent interest (compounded monthly). (Interest rates for borrowing money are generally higher than they'll give you for saving money.) Here's how it works: Your payment amount would be $106.26 per month. In five years, you would make 60 payments, right? But notice how much more than the original $5,000 you have to pay back to the bank:

Payment Amount

$106.26

Number of Payments

60

Amount to Pay Back

$6,375.60

That extra $1,375.60 was the interest you paid! That's why banks take such an interest in serving you. J. Reuben Clark described the darker side of interest like this:

> Once in debt, interest is your companion every minute of the day and night; you cannot shun it or slip away from it; you cannot dismiss it; it yields neither to entreaties, demands, or orders; and whenever you get in its way or cross its course or fail to meet its demands, it crushes you.
>
> So much for the interest we pay. Whoever borrows should understand what interest is; it is with them every minute of the day and night. (Conference Report, April 1938, pp. 102–3)

So, would you rather be paying interest or earning it?

Now, let's get back to a happier topic. Just for fun, I thought I'd make you a little chart so you can better grasp the time value of money. Let's say you want to have a million dollars when you retire at age 65. How much do you have to deposit each month, starting today? (We'll use examples of the bank paying 5 percent or 8 percent interest, compounded monthly.)

Years to retirement	Amount to deposit at 5 percent interest	Amount to deposit at 8 percent interest	Amount you'll have at retirement
50	374.74	126.09	1,000,000.00
45	493.54	189.63	1,000,000.00
40	655.39	286.51	1,000,000.00
35	880.33	436.03	1,000,000.00
30	1201.61	671.03	1,000,000.00
25	1679.45	1051.72	1,000,000.00
20	2433.21	1698.09	1,000,000.00
15	3741.76	2890.46	1,000,000.00
10	6440.21	5466.53	1,000,000.00
5	14706.45	13612.51	1,000,000.00
1	81450.55	80337.09	1,000,000.00

Which sounds easier to you, saving $126 or $375 a month right now, or waiting until you're forty-five years old to think about retirement (like most people) and having to save $1698 or $2433 a month? That's why starting while you're young with so many years ahead is important.

What if you don't have $375 or $126 each month? Then start now with whatever you can. The day will come when you'll be able to increase the amount of each deposit and still reach your goals. Most people don't even have goals. A 1989 study of 100 sixty-five-year-olds done by the US Department of Commerce revealed that only 6 out of 100 had incomes of over $25,000. They didn't plan to fail, they just failed to plan. Take another step toward becoming a most remarkable and unusual teenager and start a savings plan.

The great temptation, when you get a little money, is to go out and spend it all. Save at least a little, okay? There are a million voices out there that want your money. They say things like, "You owe it to yourself to buy this," and "Look how much you'll save," when what they really want you to do is owe the money to them so they can save it. The salespeople and retailers have twisted our vocabulary so much that when we get a bargain we brag to our friends, "Look how much I saved!" Saved? We didn't save anything. We spent something. We buy a car and say, "My payments are only $199 a month!" Yeah, but for how many months? And how much will we pay in interest? And what will our car look like in five years?

Keeping more of your money and putting it away is just another one of those things that feels not so good now, but will feel great later. To quote Dennis R. Deaton's grandmother: "You have mastered yourself when you can hear something bad about another person and not spread it; when you can receive injury or insult and not return it; when you can have money in your pocket and not spend it."

Most of us will have a job for most of our lives, so find something to do that you love. Solve your boss's problems, and solve some of your own by saving what you earn. This chapter has been a really brief introduction to a few career and financial ideas, just enough to get you "interested." I hope you'll ask your career counselor, math teacher, and bank officer for more details. They'll be surprised at what a forward-looking, incredible teenager you are.

Thanks for sticking with me and reading this far. I'll see you in sixth period, or maybe later at Honkin' Burger.

ROMANCE 101

What love's got to do with it

*There is only one kind of love, but
there are one thousand imitations.*

—François de la Rochefoucauld

I have some great memories of elementary school. When we were really young, we used to argue back and forth about who was better, boys or girls. When we got older, we used to tease the girls, knowing full well that deep down we wanted them to admire us and like us. We hoped they would see us make a great shot or score a touchdown. Years passed, and eventually we got to high school. We didn't tease the girls at recess anymore, but we still wanted them to admire us. High school romances can be so much fun. What is more fun than sitting in all your classes on the first day of school and deciding who to have a crush on? And what can compare to the feeling of finding out that somebody likes you?

Along with all these new experiences, I remember when I signed up for my first high school health class. I heard that once we got past all the lessons about drugs and alcohol and tobacco, we were going to talk a little bit about dating and, of course, sex. I was curious, as I guess every ninth grader was, but I didn't get what I expected.

We learned all about the various body parts and what they do, but nothing about the emotional part. We had lots of charts and pictures, but we got nothing about commitment or devotion or caring deeply about another person. I thought we were going to hear about love; what I got instead was an anatomy lesson. I was disappointed.

Perhaps I was a little naive. Aren't love and sex the same thing? It seems that these days, we hear a lot more about sex and a lot less about love. Aren't they supposed to be together? Don't all the songs on the radio call it "making love"? Is real love involved, or is that just what they call it? Aren't you supposed to really love somebody before you have sex? Which led me to ask (along with Tina Turner), "What's love got to do with it?"

THE CONFUSION

Teenagers today are in a tough position because there are so many voices telling them what they should or shouldn't do, and it's obvious that the adults giving the advice aren't in agreement, either. Most adults are reluctant to draw a definite line and say, "This is right, and this is wrong." Once you've heard what the Democrats think, what the Republicans think, what the liberals think, what the conservatives think, what the health teachers think, what the talk-show hosts think, what 90210 thinks, what your parents think, and what your friends think, you have to put it all together and decide what *you* think.

How do you decide what you think? What do you start with? Well, you start with what you know. You start not with opinions, but with facts. And then you can form your own opinion based on the facts. No matter what our political views or religious background, there are certain things that are not in dispute. I give teenagers enough credit to believe that when they have the facts, they can make their own good decisions.

THE FACTS

Fact One: Not everyone is doing it.

While it may seem from television and radio that "everyone does it," it's just not true. Many teenagers are not going along with the crowd, but have made a conscious decision to practice sexual abstinence. One news report I saw back in 1994 showed over 200,000 pledge cards with the phrase "True Love Waits" being "planted" in the grass on the National Mall in Washington, D.C. Each one represented a teenager who took a pledge to wait until he or she was married to have sex. Many schools have adopted sex education programs advocating abstinence, such as "Sex Respect," "Facing Reality," "Me, My World, My Future," and "Reasonable Reasons to Wait." Another report I read stated that almost 65 percent of all high school females under age eighteen are virgins.

NBA basketball star A. C. Green is thirty-four years old and not married. In a May 19, 1997, *U.S. News and World Report* article he stated:

> I am still a virgin. Abstaining from extramarital sex is one of the most unpopular things a person can do, much less talk about. From a sheer numbers standpoint, it can be a lonely cause, but that doesn't mean it's not right. I abstain as an adult for the same reasons I did as a teen—the principle doesn't change, or the feeling of self-respect I get. My fellow ballplayers

do not tell me, "You are crazy"–it's more that they think I'm being unrealistic. It's ironic, but the guys who are parents–and especially the guys who have daughters–tend to look at sex before marriage a lot more carefully now.

A. C. Green has produced a video called "It Ain't Worth It" in which he joins with "The Admiral" David Robinson of the San Antonio Spurs and other NBA and NFL stars to promote the message of abstinence. (To find out more, look him up at www.acgreen.com or call 1–800-ACYOUTH.)

The fact is, not everybody is doing it, and you don't have to do it either. Period.

Fact Two: There is no such thing as completely "safe sex."

The AIDS crisis has forced us to look more carefully at teenage sex and all STDs (sexually transmitted diseases) not just as a social problem but as a matter of life and death. While using a condom can *reduce* the risk of contracting an STD, it cannot *eliminate* the risk. One study showed the failure rate on condoms to be 15.7 percent! Among young, unmarried, minority women, the failure rate climbs to 36.3 percent! You might say, "Well, I'm willing to take my chances." Really? If you were booked on a flight where you knew that fifteen out of a hundred people might not make it to their destination alive, would you still get on board? Or would you have sex with someone who you knew had AIDS even if you were using a condom?

Actually, I don't care what all the studies say. A few years ago, I knew two different guys at my office who were both trying to prevent their wives from becoming

WHAT LOVE'S GOT TO DO WITH IT

pregnant by using condoms. You know what we call them now? Fathers.

Still another way to learn the truth is to go to a drugstore and look at the fine print on the condom packages. Can you find even one that says "Guaranteed to prevent pregnancy and STDs"? No, and you never will. They can reduce the risk, but they cannot eliminate the risk. And that's not my opinion, that's a fact.

Fact Three: Many teenagers regret having sex too soon.

This isn't a hard one to verify. Just ask them. A January 1998 Reuters News Service story reported: "People who have sex before age 16 say love is rarely a motive and later regret losing their virginity so young." The report also stated that "Men seek out their first sexual experience out of curiosity whereas women more often yield to peer pressure." (Are curiosity and peer pressure good reasons to lose your virginity? I ask again, "What's love got to do with it?") Continuing with the article: "Whatever the explanation, these results show that a substantial proportion of young women regret early intercourse. . . . One factor is that women who have sex early bear most of the responsibility for an unwanted pregnancy. Women also face a bigger risk of contracting sexually transmitted diseases" (*Deseret News,* January 1–2, 1998, p. A11).

I doubt you will ever find anyone who will say, "I'm so glad I had sex when I was a teenager." And even if they do, ask them if they regret it on the day they're getting married—to someone else.

Fact Four: Children born to teenage mothers face numerous risks.

The January 1995 issue of "Teen Talk," published by the U.S. Department of Health and Human Services, states, "Babies of young, teen mothers are more likely to be born with serious health problems." In addition to health concerns, teen mothers are generally not prepared for the demands of motherhood. Having a child is expensive, requiring food, diapers, clothing and medical care in addition to the emotional needs of almost unlimited time, attention, and love. How can all of those things be provided when children of teenage mothers are about five times more likely to be raised in poverty?

Recently, I was invited to speak to a group of "at risk" youth. Before my presentation, I listened to a panel of teen mothers answer questions. Their stories tore me apart. One of the high school students asked one of the mothers, "Why didn't you use birth control?" Her answer was very revealing. She said, "I *wanted* to get pregnant. I wanted a baby. I wanted to feel needed."

What made me sad about her answer was that it revealed her youth and lack of maturity. It was  totally selfish. Where was the love for the baby? Her answer completely ignored the baby's future. She wanted a baby to meet *her* needs. But what about the baby's needs? Will the baby have a home? How about the father—will he be around? Will he be able to support a wife and child if he's also a teenager? Will the mother be able to graduate from high school? If not, what kind of job can she get to support her new child? What kind of educational and growth opportunities will this child have? When you ponder these problems you begin to understand why President Clinton called teenage pregnancy the nation's most serious social problem.

Are these "scare tactics"? Well, if the truth scares you, I guess they are. I don't think they're "tactics," though; they're just the truth. Wouldn't you rather know the truth before making such an important decision? If you were about to step in front of an oncoming train, and someone warned you that you might get killed, would you accuse that person of using "scare tactics"? Folks, sometimes the truth is scary, and what I've written is the truth.

TRUTH AND CONSEQUENCES

This is America, the land of opportunity. We're free to think and choose for ourselves. We can go anywhere, do anything, and become anything we set our hearts on. There's one freedom, however, that neither the Constitution nor anyone else can guarantee, and that's the freedom to choose the consequences of what we do. For example, we are completely free to jump off the roof, but we are not free to choose whether the law of gravity will apply to us. It will, and we will fall.

One of the sure signs that you are becoming a mature person is your ability to link *cause* and *consequence*. It's your ability to look at a decision and see beyond the short-term effects into the future. It's asking yourself, "If I do this now, what are the possible consequences? How will I feel about it in five years, or ten years, or twenty years? Would I want my children to make the same decision?" If you can do this and not let your answers be tainted by your emotions or by what you hope will happen, you're on your way to adulthood. Everything you do has consequences. Everything. So choose wisely.

One of the problems with television programs is they don't very often show consequences. Instead, they show us a fantasy land where all the problems are solved in half an hour (minus commercials). They show us a set of glamorous actors and actresses who always wear the best clothes, who always have the sun glistening off their perfect hair, who always drive the coolest cars with no dents or rust, and who always say and do the cleverest things. What's wrong with this? It's not at all like real life. It's fake. I like what one reporter wrote about a popular show:

> UNREAL LIFE: When "Beverly Hills, 90210" premiered 2 1/2 years ago, Fox told everyone that what would make this show special was that—despite its ritzy setting—it was about real kids with real problems.
>
> Yeah, like young David, who had to decide whether to attend the funeral of his friend's father—who was killed by the mob—or go to a recording session with the record company that just signed him.
>
> That sort of thing was always happening to me when I was in high school. (Scott D. Pierce, *Deseret News*, February 24–25, 1993, p. C6)

Some of these soaps and sitcoms not only neglect to show the consequences of the characters' actions, they may actually lead young viewers to believe there are no consequences. The characters on TV mess around, fool around, and sleep around like an endless game of musical beds, and by next week at 7:00, everything's okay. Is that real life? Can you have casual sex with multiple partners and not leave behind a devastating wake of broken hearts, hurt feelings, and unintended pregnancies or STDs whose effects may last for years? And if you can, what's love got to do with it? Nothing!

Said one CBS-TV producer, "I'm not a person who believes that TV is there to educate and teach moral lessons. I don't think that's our job." Obviously not. But could you at least have the decency to show that actions have consequences? One young woman expressed it like this: "It's not a pretty picture. It's not a TV soap opera either. The reality of pregnancy outside of marriage is scary and lonely. To have premarital sex was my choice one hot June night, forcing many decisions I thought I would never have to make. Those decisions radically changed my life."

Many years ago I saw a show where a college-age young man went on a date. When he returned, his roommates asked him, "Well, did you score?" That was their only question. They didn't say, "What's she like? Is she nice? Did you have fun being together? What does she like to do? Do you have a lot to talk about? How do you feel about her?" They just wanted to know if he "scored." Sex wasn't regarded as personal or beautiful, to be saved for a very special person; it was reduced to a mark on a scorecard. Is that all it is to you? If you give yourself to someone, is that all you want it to mean to them?

MAKING YOUR CHOICE

The most important person involved in this whole discussion, and the one all this research is for, is the one looking at these words right now. It's you. So . . . what will *you* do? This is one decision that is probably better to make when you are sane, awake, and thinking straight. Some people don't spend any time at all making this huge life decision. They wait until they're making out in the backseat of a car where their emotions and passions are in control. Not smart. Make the decision when your brain is in control. The consequences of this decision will be with you your whole life!

When I have a really tough decision to make, I like to write down all the pros and cons. Somehow it's easier to see things clearly when they are written in black and white. Let's try it using teenage sex as an example:

Decision I can control	Consequences I can't control
Having sex now	Loss of virginity
	Possibility of pregnancy
	New decisions to make:
	Put the baby up for adoption?
	Get married?
	Leave school and get a job?
	Go on welfare?
	Possibility of contracting an STD
	Problem of paying for treatments
	Possibility of long-term health consequences
	Possibility of getting pregnant and getting an STD
	All of the above
Not having sex now	Retain my virginity
	Those interested in me for sex might lose interest
	Those who love me just for me will stay

There it is in black and white. What do you think? Can you see how it makes things clearer when you write them out? Choices have consequences, and we must want the consequences of what we choose. The old saying is, "When you pick up one end of the stick, you pick up the other." What's on the other end of the stick? Well, as we've seen above, there are many possible consequences of having sex. The one sure thing about teenage sex is that you may be in for problems you don't know how to handle.

A chart like this is helpful, or you may just want to ask yourself a few questions as you evaluate your decision, and try to see cause and consequence. A Department of Health and Human Services brochure recommends considering these:

> Is having sex in agreement with my own moral values?
>
> Would my parents approve of my having sex now?
>
> If I have a child, am I responsible enough to provide for its emotional and financial support?
>
> If the relationship breaks up, will I be glad I had sex with this person?
>
> Am I sure no one is pushing me to have sex?
>
> Am I absolutely sure my partner is not infected with an STD including AIDS?

Many teens never ponder these questions or make a chart similar to the one above. Instead, they ask one three-word question: "Is it fun?" It's a short-term, immature approach to decision making, but many use it. Others may say, "Well, those bad things happen to some people, but they're not going to happen to me." Those with this attitude are taking an awful gamble. *No moment of pleasure is worth dying for.* Make sure you understand the difference between having fun now and dealing with the possible consequences of the "fun" later.

As you make your choice, be informed. Make the choice regardless of what you think "everybody is doing." You're not "everybody." You're someone unique and special. Make the decision as someone of infinite worth, because you are.

WHAT LOVE'S GOT TO DO WITH IT

Unfortunately, when we talk about sex, we often forget what should be the most important part—love. Sex without love is hollow and meaningless. Sex without love is lust. We often get love and lust confused.

Here comes a bold statement, are you ready? *Men and women are different.* Are you shocked? Take a deep breath and go on. I know that's a radical statement, but we're realizing that we are different in *many* ways, not just physically. Sometimes we're so far apart, it's like we're from different planets! In fact, one of the most successful books ever written about male-female relationships is John Gray's *Men are from Mars, Women are from Venus*. Saying that we're different is not saying that one gender is better than the other. Of course not. It's just recognizing that we think, feel, and act in different ways. We are not the same (and I, for one, am delighted with the differences)!

One of the most important ways men and women are different is emotionally. We perceive things differently; we interpret things differently. Generally speaking, when a girl is being kissed by a boy, she may be thinking, "Oh, he really likes me. He really cares about me. And this is how he is showing it." Inside the boy's mind may be the thought, "Wow, this feels good. I'd like to do this again very soon." Can you see how far apart those two interpretations are? Like the distance between Mars and Venus! Here's another example: It's an old joke among newly engaged couples that, as the big day draws nearer, the bride will be thinking about the wedding day, and the groom will be thinking about the wedding night. It's not just a joke; it's true! Generally speaking, it's the way we are.

We need to put the love back into the discussions about sex. If a guy takes you on a date to see if he can "score," then real love is missing. There is only lust. But some young women want so much to be held, to be treated tenderly, to "feel" loved, that they'll give in to having sex to get the love. And many young men have learned that if they will give "love," or act in loving ways, they can get someone to go to bed with them. In short, *many young men give love to get sex, and many young women give sex to get love.*

Interestingly, if an unwanted pregnancy occurs, their real intentions are revealed. The guy who just wanted to "score" disappears, leaving the girl with a child and some life-changing decisions to make. Love is different from lust. Love would not disappear. Love is commitment and caring and sacrificing and self-restraint.

Someone who *really* loves you is concerned about you, your feelings, your dreams, and your future—not just your body.

Whenever you have sex with someone, you give a part of your self away. We can talk all about "safe sex" and "protection," but there's no drugstore protection for a broken heart. Sex without love is a heartbreaking experience. True love waits.

WHAT YOUR AUTHOR THINKS

Gee, can you tell? I think you know. I believe the best decision you can make is abstaining from sex before marriage. I don't believe anything good comes from teens having sex. There are just too many negative consequences. So many teens have chosen to experiment with sex too soon, and they inevitably suffer the consequences. They find they have some very adult problems to deal with all of a sudden. They have given away their youth for a moment of pleasure.

There will be a time when you will want to take on the responsibilities of sexual activity and parenthood. But not now. I believe you should be young and have fun. And you can have plenty of fun and explore all that life has to offer without having sex.

I'm not saying to you, "Don't do what I did." I'm saying, "I abstained, and it's one of the reasons my marriage is happy." I waited until I was married, and you can too. So, you know what your author thinks; what will you do? It's your turn to take a stand. As the old saying goes, "If you don't stand for something, you could fall for anything." My advice is to free yourself from this whole debate. Free yourself from trying to decide, should I or shouldn't I? Free yourself from all the pressures and just say, "I'm waiting, I'm waiting, I'm waiting." You have a right to say no. You can "just say no" to drugs, you can "just say no" to violence, and you can "just say no" to premarital sex.

Remember, you're not saying no because sex is bad, but because it's so good, so personal, and so special that you have the maturity and courage to say, "No. I'm waiting until later." Once you've made your decision, you don't have to make it again and again. You've already decided. You're saying to yourself and to the world, "What I have to give is so valuable that I guard it very carefully. I don't give it out to just anybody. I don't share my affections like free samples at the grocery store."

Around Christmastime, people place beautiful gifts under the tree and postpone opening them until Christmas morning. Some are tempted to sneak in and open all their presents before Christmas, but it ruins the fun and the anticipation. To me, experimenting too early with sex is like opening all your presents before Christmas. It's not nearly as nice. You see, you are working on a wonderful gift. You've been working on it since you were born, and only you can give it! You don't want to share it until the time is just right. On some exciting future day, you'll be able to give this gift to someone else. The gift you've been working on all your life is *you*.

Somewhere out there is your future husband or wife. They're probably going to school, just like you. They probably watch a lot of the same shows, struggle in classes, and face a lot of pressures, just like you. Wouldn't it be fun to look in a crystal ball and see what they're doing right now? It sure would be nice. Unfortunately, we don't have a crystal ball, so let's ask a different question: What do you *hope* they're doing? Are they dating? Are they feeling the pressure to have sex because "everyone is doing it"? If you could talk to them now, what would you say? What advice would you give them? Do you hope that they are saving themselves for you? And what if they could talk back? What do you think they would say to you?

In doing research for this chapter, I came across a video called *Sex, Lies, and the Truth*. A beautiful young actress named Lakita Garth said something that really impressed me. She was a virgin and was determined to remain so until her wedding day. She can't talk to her future husband right now, because she hasn't met him yet. But she expresses her love to him every day. Every time she guards her virginity and says "no" to casual sex, she is saying, "I love you." He hasn't heard her say it yet, but on their wedding day, she plans to say to her new husband, "I loved you before I ever knew you. And I saved myself just for you."

That, my friend, is what love's got to do with it.

Seventh Period

PREPARATION 101

How to get opportunity to knock you over

> *"I always wanted to be somebody.*
> *I guess I should have been*
> *more specific."*
>
> —Lily Tomlin

S omeday you'll graduate. You'll be done with high school. Are you excited about that? You should be. As that day draws near, you'll be afflicted with a bad case of the twelfth-grade malady they call "Senioritis." Symptoms include a great desire to get out of high school and do something new! You may even sit in class and dream of graduation.

Can you imagine it? You'll rent that cap and gown thing, you'll walk down the aisle, and then you'll be a high school graduate, right? Yee-haw! Then what? Well, you wear shorts, sit around, guzzle pop, and watch ESPN. Right? Wrong! Well, okay, maybe for a day or two, but take a close look at the program they'll pass out at graduation. You might notice another word on there. (Hint: it starts with a "C.") *Commencement*. To *commence* is to start. Graduation isn't the end, it's just the beginning! Your life is just getting started, my friend.

Up until graduation, your life has been like a train, and all you've had to do was follow the track. In sixth grade, if someone asked you what you were doing with your life, you would have responded with the brilliant phrase, "Huh?" You were just following the track, going grade by grade, doing what everyone else was doing. The track took you through elementary school, junior high, and high school. You knew exactly what you'd be doing year after year, but suddenly, the track ends. You've grown out of your "choo-choo," and now you can trade it in for an F-16, engage the afterburners, and go anywhere you want at Mach 2.

So what are your plans? Airplanes need flight plans, you know. The wild blue yonder is big. This may seem like a strange time to retell the Bible story of David and Goliath, but stay tuned. When David was preparing to meet Goliath, he "chose him five smooth stones out of the brook" and put them in his bag (1 Samuel 17:40). Later, when he confronted Goliath, he "put his hand in his bag, and took thence a stone" (verse 49). The first stone he picked and hurled with his sling was the next thing that went through Goliath's head, so to speak.

You know the story, but here's a question you may never have thought of before. What if David had missed? What if his stone had flown over Goliath's head? (Can't you just hear Goliath's army chanting, "*Air rock, air rock.*") Well, David had four other stones in his bag, and he would have loaded one of them. You see, *David had backup plans.* He had Plan A, Plan B, Plan C, Plan D, and Plan E.

When you graduate, you'll be faced with a formidable giant called "the future." You'll need backup plans too. They say that opportunity only knocks once. I disagree. Opportunity doesn't *knock*. You *create* it by being prepared. Opportunity is not just "being in the right place at the right time," but being prepared before you get to the right place at the right time. One of the best definitions of *luck* I've ever heard is this: "Luck is when preparation meets opportunity." It's not an opportunity unless you're prepared to accept it.

David's stone knocked Goliath over. I'd like to show you how to get opportunity not only to knock but to knock you over too.

PLAN YOUR FUNERAL NOW!

This may sound like a strange time in your life to start thinking about your funeral, but hear me out. Once I participated in a goal-setting workshop with an impressive group of teenage peer counselors. At the beginning of my seminar, I asked them to write what they would like to have said about them at their funerals. After some rather serious thought, they wrote their feelings. When they were finished, a few brave ones read their personal "epitaphs" to the group. What they said was interesting, but what they *didn't* say was even more interesting. All of them mentioned being a parent: "She was a wonderful wife and mother," or "He was a father who spent time with his children." All of them mentioned service, too: "He was always there to help anyone who needed him," and "She was always helping others." After the reading, we had a group discussion about what people didn't say. We noticed that not one person mentioned how much money they had made or even what kind of career they'd had. No one mentioned cars or sport-utility vehicles or possessions of any kind. Instead, these top-notch teenagers wrote about the things that really matter: family, friends, and helping others. (Once again, I learned to never underestimate teenagers.)

This is why I suggest thinking ahead to your death to plan your life. When you're thinking about your life at the last, it helps you decide what ought to come first. At the end of the seminar, I asked the group to erase the word *Epitaph* at the top of their papers and replace it with the words *Mission Statement*. "What you have just written," I told them, "is your mission in life. It's what you want your life to mean. It's the answer to the question, 'What is my life for?'" (You may want to go back and change a few things from past tense to future tense, of course. For example, change "He was a good dad" to "He *will be* a good dad," and so on.)

In writing this, I'm afraid that some might say, "Are you seriously talking to teenagers about mission statements?" You see, most people don't even think about this kind of thing until they are much older. They wait until their midlife crisis to start asking what life is all about. They spend more time planning a friend's surprise party than they do planning their own life! And what they get is one surprise after another because they never decided what to do with their time.

You can be different. You *are* different. You're a teenager reading a book, for crying out loud! You can ask the hard questions now and discover your purpose while you're young.

Can mission statements change? Of course they can. You still have a lot of self-discovery to do. As you learn and experience new things, you may go off in another direction than you thought. That's okay. Generally, however, the things that are most important in life stay most important.

One of my heroes is our former First Lady, Barbara Bush. She spoke to graduates at the all-women Wellesley College in Massachusetts and asked them to look ahead to their funeral when planning their lives. The Associated Press reported:

> But while urging the graduates to pursue professional careers, if they so choose, Mrs. Bush warned, "At the end of your life, you will never regret not having passed one more test, winning one more verdict, or not closing one more deal. You will regret time not spent with a husband, a child, a friend, or a parent." (*The Daily Herald,* June 2, 1990)

Mrs. Bush is right! No one is going to look back on life and say, "Oh, I wish I'd spent more time at the office!" Instead, they'll be thinking of life's most important things: family, friends, and service. What will you look back on? Someone once said, "Your life is God's gift to you; what you do with your life is your gift to God." Make your life a gift to God.

There's a long time (we hope) between now and your funeral, but today is the day to write your epitaph. Once you know what your life is about, or what you want it to be about, decisions about how to spend your time are easier to make. Opportunity knocks loudest for those who know where they're going.

UNPLUG THE PLUG-IN DRUG

Here's another thing you can do to create opportunities. Let's say you're at home one summer day, and you hear the doorbell ring. You stand up from the couch, take another bite of your burrito, and walk to the door. Now you're standing face to face with a door-to-door salesman. He tells you he has something to offer that will save you money, give you more time, help you reach your dreams, and change your life. What would you say? "Yeah, right, what is it, a treadmill?"

"No," he responds, "it's free."

"Is it multilevel marketing?" you ask.

He stops, looks both ways, leans toward you, and softly whispers, "Unplug your television." Then he walks away. You're left standing there wide-eyed and open-mouthed (revealing your half-chewed burrito). Well, would you believe it? Would you give it any thought? Or would you go right back and finish watching *Daze of Our Lives?*

According to an organization called TV-Free America, the average American watches four hours of television each day. *Four hours.* How pathetic. This makes me sick because I haven't met a teenager yet who didn't have dreams. I bet every one of you out there reading this book has something you like to do and would like to be able to do even better. It may be sports or music or writing or singing or a million other things.

Can you imagine if you spent four hours a day working on your dream instead of watching TV? Can you imagine how much of a difference that would make in only one month?

When I decided to write my first book, I had to make an interesting decision. It wasn't because of a mysterious door-to-door salesman, but the impact was the same. I realized that if I were ever to get my book done, I would have to set aside a few hours each day to write. Because I had a full-time job, the only time of day I could think of to spend on my writing was really early in the morning. It's a perfect time because people don't bother you early in the morning; they don't ring your doorbell to borrow sugar, and they don't call on the phone to gab. Most people are still asleep! I decided to start getting up at 5:00 A.M. Then I realized that I was going to have to go to bed a little earlier, sacrificing my nightly ritual. Could I possibly get along without Letterman and Leno? What if someone asked me if I'd seen the "Top Ten" and I had to say no? Social disaster!

But a man's gotta do what a man's gotta do. So I traded my least productive hours, the hours I spent in front of the TV, for my most productive hours. I went to bed at 10:00 and got up at 5:00. When the alarm went off it was still dark outside, but I'd quickly shower and dress, and then I'd grab my laptop computer and head to my office. Walking through the chilly air from the dark parking lot to the building, I recited in my mind a verse from Longfellow as I tried to convince myself that it was worth it to get up this early:

The heights by great men reached and kept
Were not attained by sudden flight,
But they, while their companions slept,
Were toiling upward in the night.

For two hours each morning, I'd sit at the computer. Some mornings, I'd get out a few pages; other mornings, only a paragraph. It was hard. At times it was discouraging. Sometimes, when that alarm went off, I wanted to blow it away with a shotgun. But I kept at it. You know, at the end of the first month, I had thirty-five single-spaced pages of material. I was amazed! Two hours a day for a month really adds up. The next thing I did was contact a publisher and send them those thirty-five pages. To my delight, the publisher was interested, and in two more months, my book was accepted for publication. I couldn't believe it! The next fall I walked into a bookstore and saw my book on the shelf. My life changed forever! All because I turned off the TV.

Now, what if I had kept my old routine for those three months? What would I have had to show for it? Anything? Well, maybe I could've remembered a few jokes from Letterman and Leno, but that's about it. Instead, *I had written a book,* a dream I had had since I was sixteen.

What about you? Are you working on your dreams, or are you spending four hours a day watching other people live their dreams on TV? Aside from being full of sex, violence, and trash, much of television is a colossal waste of time—time that you could be using to become better at what you do. Watching television will probably not help you create opportunities (unless you want to be a TV critic). Why not use your time to expand your mind and build your brain?

The fact is, you already have two talents that can open doors of opportunity for you all over the world. This story, from the life of Dr. Jean Louis Rodolphe Agassiz (1807-1873), is one that I love to tell whenever I speak at school assemblies.

> One night in London, at the conclusion of a lecture by the distinguished naturalist Dr. Louis Agassiz, a woman complained to him that she "had never had a chance." In response to her complaint, he replied: "Do you say, madam, you never had a chance? What do you do?"
>
> "I am single and help my sister run a boardinghouse."
>
> "What do you do?" he asked.
>
> "I skin potatoes and chop onions."
>
> He said, "Madam, where do you sit during these interesting but homely duties?"
>
> "On the bottom step of the kitchen stairs."
>
> "Where do your feet rest?"
>
> "On the glazed brick."
>
> "What is glazed brick?"
>
> "I don't know, sir."
>
> He said, "How long have you been sitting there?"
>
> She said, "Fifteen years."
>
> "Madam, here is my personal card," said Dr. Agassiz. "Would you kindly write me a letter concerning the nature of a glazed brick?"
>
> She took him seriously. She went home

and explored the dictionary and discovered that a brick was a piece of baked clay. That definition seemed too simple to send to Dr. Agassiz, so after the dishes were washed, she went to the library and in an encyclopedia read that a glazed brick is vitrified kaolin and hydrous aluminum silicate. She didn't know what that meant, but she was curious and found out. She took the word *vitrified* and read all she could find about it. Then she visited museums. She moved out of the basement of her life and into a new world on the wings of *vitrified*. And having started, she took the word *hydrous,* studied geology, and went back in her studies to the time when God started the world and laid the clay beds. One afternoon she went to a brickyard, where she found the history of more than 120 kinds of bricks and tiles, and why there have to be so many. Then she sat down and wrote thirty-six pages on the subject of glazed brick and tile.

Back came the letter from Dr. Agassiz: "Dear Madam, this is the best article I have ever seen on the subject. If you will kindly change the three words marked with asterisks I will have it published and pay you for it."

A short time later there came a letter that brought $250, and penciled on the bottom of this letter was this query: "What was under those bricks?" She had learned the value of time and answered with a single word: "Ants." He wrote back and said, "Tell me about the ants."

She began to study ants. She found there were between eighteen hundred and twenty-five hundred different kinds. There are ants so tiny you could put three head-to-head on a pin and have standing room left over for other ants; ants an inch long that march in solid armies half a mile wide, driving everything ahead of them; ants that are blind; ants that get wings on the afternoon of the day they die; ants that build anthills so tiny that you can cover one with a lady's silver thimble; peasant ants that keep cows to milk, and then deliver the fresh milk to the apartment house of the aristocratic ants of the neighborhood.

After wide reading, much microscopic work, and deep study, the spinster sat down and wrote Dr. Agassiz 360 pages on the subject. He published the book and sent her the money, and she went to visit all the lands of her dreams on the proceeds of her work. (Marion D. Hanks, *The Gift of Self*, Bookcraft, Inc., 1974, pp. 151–53)

Dr. Agassiz was a great teacher. He didn't make this woman attend a class where some instructor would fill her full of facts about ants and bricks. He simply let her discover for herself that she already had all the talent she needed to make something wonderful of her life: she could read, and she could write.

So, how do you get opportunity to knock you over? Well, for one thing, you keep learning. You make it a habit to always be learning something new. Instead of a tendency for television, you develop a bias for books.

And not just any books. Read good books. There's plenty of trash out there, so leave it in the literary dumpster. Mark Twain once said, "The man who does not read good books has no advantage over the man who can't read them." In other words, if you're going to read, be choosy. Read the things that will make you a better employee, a better family member, and a more interesting person.

THEN I'LL BE HAPPY!

Many teenagers think that happiness comes when everything in life is just perfect. Actually, it doesn't work that way. Happiness is a choice. People are happy because they choose to be, in spite of all the problems they have. If you think you have to wait until everything is perfect to be happy, you're going to wait forever! I like the old Chinese proverb: "He who waits for roast duck to fly into mouth must wait a long time." Waiting to be happy until everything is perfect is like waiting for that roast duck to fly into your face.

As you grow older, the temptation will be to attach an event to your happiness. "As soon as I graduate, I'll be happy" becomes "As soon as I get a job, I'll be happy" which becomes "As soon as I'm married, I'll be happy" which changes to "As soon as the kids are grown, I'll be happy" which evolves into "As soon as I can retire, I'll be happy" which leads to "As soon as I'm dead, I'll be happy."

I don't know about you, but I'm a little too impatient to wait until I'm dead to be happy. Why don't we start being happy right now? It all comes down to a choice.

George Bernard Shaw said: "People are always

blaming their circumstances for what they are. I don't believe in circumstances. The people who get on in this world are the people who get up and look for the circumstances they want, and, if they can't find them, make them."

Recently I read a story about a restaurant manager who was always in a good mood. One of his friends asked him how he always managed to stay so happy. He replied, "Each morning I wake up and say to myself, 'You have two choices today. You can choose to be in a good mood or you can choose to be in a bad mood.' I choose to be in a good mood. Each time something bad happens, I can choose to be a victim or I can choose to learn from it. I choose to learn from it. Every time someone comes to me complaining, I can choose to accept their complaining or I can point out the positive side of life. I choose the positive side of life."

Several years later, this man was held up at gunpoint and shot. How did he react to that situation? I mean, being in a good mood in the morning is one thing—but what kind of mood are you in after you've been shot? He continued:

> As I lay on the floor, I remembered that I had two choices: I could choose to live, or I could choose to die. I chose to live. . . . When they wheeled me into the emergency room and I saw the expressions on the faces of the doctors and nurses, I got really scared. In their eyes, I read, "He's a dead man." I knew I needed to take action. . . . There was a big burly nurse shouting questions at me. She

asked if I was allergic to anything. "Yes," I replied. The doctors and nurses stopped working as they waited for my reply. I took a deep breath and yelled, "Bullets!" Over their laughter, I told them, "I am choosing to live. Operate on me as if I am alive, not dead." (*Chicken Soup for the Soul at Work,* Health Communications, Inc., 1996, pp. 211–13)

That's the power of choosing. From now on, whenever you're tempted to say "He made me mad" or "She made me unhappy," I want you to remember that you get to choose. Sure, he did what he did, but you chose to be unhappy about it. You could have chosen differently. Easier said than done? For sure. But you get to decide. You cannot choose what happens to you, but you can always choose how you respond to what happens to you. That's a freedom no one can take away.

In other words, don't wait for happiness to fly into your mouth (unless you see a flock of roast duck circling overhead). Instead, just be happy anyway.

PRESCRIPTION FOR LONG-TERM HAPPINESS: MAKE A DIFFERENCE

Many people go through cycles in life. They may work for many years on the assumption that money is what will make them happy. They'll sacrifice almost everything for a career. They'll slave and sweat and work and hardly have time for anything else. A number of these people will actually achieve what they thought they wanted. They'll get money. And then they'll make a startling discovery: It didn't make them happy.

Others might set out on a quest for fame. They'll

work and sweat and slave in their professions seeking to be well known. They want the world to tell them they're somebody! The funny thing is, as soon as everyone knows who they are, they wear sunglasses in public to avoid being recognized. They, like those who go after the almighty dollar, discover that it didn't make them happy either. Oh, sure, they've had their moments of fame, and no doubt that's a rush, but it's nothing to build a life on. Sometimes those who seem to "have it all" throw their lives away on drugs (like John Belushi or Chris Farley). What a tragedy! Wasn't their fame and money enough? I guess not.

Sooner or later, all of us discover that the only pursuit that brings the long-term, peaceful kind of happiness is serving others. It's in trying to make a difference. (If you can learn this great lesson now, you'll avoid a lot of wasted time later.) When you know that someone will smile, or laugh, or have a better day because of you, it's almost impossible not to smile inside. That's long-term happiness. Ralph Waldo Emerson defined it like this:

> To laugh often and much: To win the respect of intelligent people and the affection of children, to earn the appreciation of honest critics and endure the betrayal of false friends; to appreciate beauty, to find the best in others, to leave the world a bit better whether by a healthy child, a garden patch, or a redeemed social condition; to know even one life has breathed easier because you lived. This is to have succeeded. (As quoted in *The Forbes Book of Business Quotations,* ed. Ted Goodman, Black Dog and Leventhal Publishers, Inc., 1997, p. 800)

Just like we talked about in Second Period, the way to find yourself is to forget yourself and make a difference. Whatever you become in life, and wherever you go (and you'll go far), don't forget it's all about people. Find a way to make a difference in the lives of people. Make them better, happier, stronger, or smarter. The satisfaction it brings is worth more than money and fame.

You want opportunities? Then plan your funeral and make your epitaph wonderful. Learn all you can and never stop learning. Choose to be happy now. Serve people, and you'll make a difference.

AND NOW, THE CHEESY PART NEAR THE END

Well, I guess it's time to say good-bye. You're a pretty amazing teenager, you know that? First of all, you're reading a book. Second, you've read all the way to the last chapter! (Is there anyone out there reading this? What's that? You're the only one? Oh well. That's about right. Ninety percent of Americans don't read past the first chapter of the books they buy.) You are a rare individual. There are so many more books out there, books much better than this one. Give your library card a workout and go check them out!

I have a lot of respect for teenagers like you. A lot of people are really worried about where the world is going. Sometimes I worry too. But if there are more young people like you out there, I think we'll be okay. This world needs you. And we all need each other.

Well, I hope you liked this long letter from a friend. I tried to write all the things I wish I'd known when I was in high school, but it seems I've left so much out! The more I learn, the more I realize how little I know.

This book had three goals; do you remember? *Learn things, have fun,* and *make changes.* So, how did we do? Did you learn things? (Write answer here—unless this is the library's book) _____. Did you have fun? _____. Did you, or will you, make changes? "What changes?" you ask. Well, let's review: First Period told you to stop worrying about being popular; Second Period told you to recognize your own potential; Third Period talked about finding the prize inside; Fourth Period told you that the orthodontia of life hurts, but it's worth it; Fifth Period told you how to get a job and get a raise; Sixth Period told you what love's got to do with it; and Seventh Period told you how to get opportunity to knock you over. Phew.

Well, I'm outta here. I have another goal. It's called, "What I Wish I'd Known in College." No, how about, "What My Retainer Taught Me about Lisping." Okay, no, "Roast Ducks and Other Airborne Oddities." Oh well. Just look for me on the shelf somewhere. Take care of yourself, and be happy! Your friend,

John Bytheway

P.S. Stop by and say hi at www.johnbytheway.com!

INDEX

Accidents, happy, 46–47
Accomplishments, 27–30, 43–46
Agassiz, Jean Louis Rodolphe, 121–23
AIDS, 98–99, 105
Ants, 122–23
Appearance, 25–27, 78
Ashton, Marvin J., 44, 53
Athletic conditioning, 65

Backup plans, 114
Barton, Bruce, 39
Beauty pageant talk, 28–29
Belushi, John, 127
Beverly Hills, 90210, 102
Books, 1, 4, 123–24, 128; on tape, 71–72
Braces, 61–63
Brick, glazed, 121–22
Brown, Les, 54–55
Bush, Barbara, 117

Carnegie, Andrew, 84–85
Changing life, 6, 14, 72–73; story about boy, 66–67
Choir, Junior, 53, 55–56
Choosing happiness, story about, 125–26
Clark, J. Reuben, 88
Classy people, 67–68
Clinton, William (U.S. President), 101
Commencement, 113
Condoms, 98–99
Consequences, 101–3; of teenage sex, 104–5
Cool Runnings, 28–29

Cracker Jack theory, 41, 57
Crawford, Cindy, 27
Cruise, Tom, 41

David and Goliath, 114
Deaton, Dennis R., 87, 90
Delegation, five levels of, 82
Differences between men and women, 106–7
Discipline, 63–66
Disney, Walt, 4
Drums, playing, 55–56

Edison, Thomas A., 73
Einstein, Albert, 41
Emerson, Ralph Waldo, 36, 127
Epitaphs, 115–17
Esquire magazine, 26
Evans, Richard L., 59
Exercise, 65, 70–71

Failure, 55
Fame, 126–27
Family, 45–46, 115–17
Farley, Chris, 127
Fear, 53
Fiddler on the Roof, 32
Foundations: for real estate, 22–24; shaky, for happiness, 24–30; solid, for happiness, 30–33
Freedom, 63–64, 101
Friends: outside your group, 10–14, 67; of opposite sex, 15; happiness not dependent on, 24–25; adult leaders as, 47–48
Funeral epitaph, 115–17

INDEX

Gandhi, Indira, 75
Garth, Lakita, 110
Getting up early, 119–20
Goals: compared to wires, 63; and discipline, 63–66; focusing on, 66–67; social, 68–69; career and financial, 69; spiritual, 69–70; physical, 70–71; intellectual, 71–72; our ability to reach, 72–73; setting, for future, 114–17
God, our relationship to, 31–32
Graduation, 113–14
Gray, John, 106
Green, A. C., 97–98

Handicapped boy, popular athlete friendly to, 13–14
Happiness, 19, 21–22, 53; not dependent on friends, 24–25; not dependent on appearance, 25–27; not dependent on accomplishments, 27–30; comes from inside, 31–33; is a choice, 124–26; comes from service, 127–28
Harper's magazine, 26
High school: frustrations about, 5; first day of, 42–43; registration, 46–47; yearbook, 48–49; track team, 49–52; choir, 53, 55–56; health class, 95–96; graduation, 113–14
Highly Informative Chart #1, 65

Ingersoll, Robert G., 19
Interest, 86–88
Intersections, 46–47
Interviews, 78–81
It Ain't Worth It, 98

James, William, 72
Jobs, 77; interviewing for, 78–81; advancing in, 81–86
Jordan, Michael, 41

Landers, Ann, 12

Learning, 4, 71–72, 123–24
Lincoln, Abraham, 31
Listening, 44–46
Litchfield, Allen, 26
Longfellow, 119–20
Love, 93; and sex, 96, 99, 106–8, 110
Luck, 115

Mandino, Og, 17, 85
Matheson, Mike, 51
Men Are from Mars, Women Are from Venus, 106
Mission statement, 116
Money, 86–90, 115, 126
Money: An Owner's Manual, 87
"Mr. C," 55–56
Muppet Show, The, 56

Observation, 68
Opportunity, creating, 114–15, 121–23

Pain, 64–65
Past, life not shaped by, 72
Patience, 37, 41, 49
Peay, John, 47
Pfeiffer, Michelle, 26
Physical fitness, 65, 70–71
Pianist, concert, 66
Popularity: and respect, 7, 10, 11, 15–18; definition of, 9–10
Pound, Ezra, 1
Pregnancy, teenage, 100–101
Princess Bride, The, 64
Prize inside, 41–42, 57
Problems, solving, for boss, 82–85

Railroad employee, story about, 84
Reading, 1, 3–4, 71, 123–24, 128
Religious beliefs, 31–32, 69–70
Respect: and popularity, 7, 15–18; how to earn, 10–12
Retirement savings, 89–90
Risks, 54
Robinson, David, 98

INDEX

Rochefoucauld, François de la, 93
Role models, 47–48

Saving money, 86–90
Self-esteem, 33–35
Self-worth, 34–37
Service, 35–36, 115, 127–28
Sex: and love, 96, 106–8;
abstaining from, 97–98, 108–10;
disease and, 98–99; regret
about early, 99; and teen
pregnancy, 100–101;
consequences of teenage, 103–6
Sex, Lies, and the Truth, 110
Shaw, George Bernard, 72, 124–25
Smith, Menlo, 82, 83
STDs (sexually transmitted
diseases), 98–99, 104, 105
Student leaders, 14–15

Talents, 41, 43–46
Television, 102–3, 118–20

Tennis player, talented, 43
Tolstoy, Leo, 26
Tomlin, Lily, 111
Track team, 49–53
TV dinner compartments, 10–11
Twain, Mark, 124
"Two-faced" people, 10, 11–12

Understanding, 44–46
"Up, Up and Away," 55–56

Williamson, Marianne, 32
Wires: and braces, 62; as goals, 63,
66–67; social, 68–69; career and
financial, 69; spiritual, 69–70;
physical, 70–71; intellectual,
71–72
Work, 85. *See also* Jobs
Writing, 119–20, 123

Yearbooks, 17–18, 48–49